Don't Fall for It

Don't Fall for It

A SHORT HISTORY OF FINANCIAL SCAMS

Ben Carlson

WILEY

For general information on our other products and services or for technical support, please contact our Customer Care Department within the United States at (800) 762-2974, outside the United States at (317) 572-3993, or fax (317) 572-4002.

Wiley publishes in a variety of print and electronic formats and by print-on-demand. Some material included with standard print versions of this book may not be included in e-books or in print-on-demand. If this book refers to media such as a CD or DVD that is not included in the version you purchased, you may download this material at http://booksupport.wiley.com. For more information about Wiley products, visit www.wiley.com.

Library of Congress Cataloging-in-Publication Data:
Names: Carlson, Benjamin Patrick, 1981- author.
Title: Don't fall for it : a short history of financial scams / Benjamin
    Patrick Carlson.
Description: Hoboken, New Jersey : John Wiley & Sons, Inc., [2020] |
    Includes bibliographical references and index.
Identifiers: LCCN 2019032942 (print) | LCCN 2019032943 (ebook) | ISBN
    9781119605164 (cloth) | ISBN 9781119605195 (adobe pdf) | ISBN
    9781119605188 (epub)
Subjects: LCSH: Swindlers and swindling–Case studies. | Fraud–Case
    studies. | Financial crimes–Case studies.
Classification: LCC HV6691 .C375 2020 (print) | LCC HV6691 (ebook) | DDC
    364.16/309–dc23
LC record available at https://lccn.loc.gov/2019032942
LC ebook record available at https://lccn.loc.gov/2019032943

Printed in the United States of America.
V10015674_111819

Contents

Introduction

The most instructive, indeed the only method of learning to bear
with dignity the vicissitude of fortune, is to recall the catastrophe of
others.

— Polybius

In 2008, a self-employed handyman named Fred Haines was wan-
dering around Wichita's Dwight D. Eisenhower airport in search of
a Nigerian man carrying two chests full of cold hard cash. After asking around and waiting for an hour or so he finally realized the $64
million inheritance he was promised in an email from Nigeria wasn't
walking off an airplane.

Over a period from 2005 to 2008, Haines mortgaged his home three
times in hopes that forking over six figures of cash would be enough to
help him receive a seven-figure inheritance from Africa. It's hard to believe the Nigerian Prince scam could be so effective but some people
just want to believe these things could be true. Haines claims the first
email he received did come off as some sort of joke or scam. Neverthe-
less, he was intrigued as the person on the other end of his correspon-
dence promised Haines he was owed tens of millions of dollars of an
inheritance that rightfully belonged to him. The scammers told Haines
his money was being moved from country to country but they needed
money along the way to grease the wheels of international law that were
overseeing the movement of his funds.

The scammers said at one point that the money had gone from Nigeria to Egypt to England to New York and once again back to Nigeria.
Haines claims to have tried to get back the money after he sent it, but
after going so deep down this rabbit hole he had convinced himself it
couldn't be a scam. "It got to the point where they were showing me
that the president of Nigeria had sent me a letter. It had his picture on

1

it and everything," Haines said. "I looked it up on the computer to see what the Nigerian president looked like, and it was him."

Then there was the email he received from Robert Mueller, Director of the FBI at the time, and a man who is now widely known for conducting an investigation of some sort on the 45th President of the United States. The subject line of this email read:

SUBJECT: FRED HAINES, CODE B-DOG

The text showed a picture of Mueller in the top left-hand corner and was littered with grammatical errors. It read:

> I receive your email and for your good and successful of operation of your account, I will advise you to look for the fee and send to them you can see that your funds is available, and everything is clear no trick on it. Looks for some one [sic] and borrow then promise to pay in three days.

You may be shocked to learn FBI Director Robert Mueller didn't actually send an email to a man in Kansas about a secret inheritance from a Nigerian prince. This was, in fact, a fake. The problem was Haines had already gone too far to give up at that point, so he held out a glimmer of hope the money was still coming. "Those Nigerians know how to talk," was his explanation for getting caught up in this fantasy. Luckily, Haines was able to recover $110,000 of what he lost in a settlement with Western Union, but others haven't been so lucky.[1]

The Airplane Game

In the late-1980s a money-making scheme called the Airplane Game was invented and the rules were quite simple. All you had to do was hand over $1,500 and the game would, in turn, give you back $12,000. What a world, right?

The reason it was called the Airplane Game is that every new player became one of eight "passengers" on a flight that also consisted of four flight attendants, two co-pilots, and a pilot. All eight passengers put in their $1,500 which went directly to the pilot as their cost of admission on the "flight." The pilot then left the game having already put in their own initial $1,500 and working their way up the ladder. The co-pilot then started two new planes, where each passenger was required to bring on a new passenger (and thus $1,500 more per person). After each successive round, the passengers moved up to flight attendants and then became pilots themselves after a turn as co-pilot, picking up their \$12,000. And the more people you brought into the game, the faster you earned your payout.[2]

This idea spread quickly to other areas across the country. It only took four days in some cases for people to move up the ranks to become a pilot and cash out. The game worked so well for so long that many players went through the process on multiple occasions, each time picking up a cool twelve grand. One man in Florida worked his way through the "airplane" nine times, making more than \$100,000 in the process.[3]

The Airplane Game didn't last because there was no business model. There were no profits, products, or revenue to speak of. In fact, the whole idea behind the airplane game was good vibes and positive thinking. Those participating at the outset assumed you could visualize your way to abundance, happiness, and wealth. And the game sounds like a sure thing until you realize the original eight passengers need to recruit 64 new passengers to get paid. Those 64 passengers then needed to turn around and recruit 512 new passengers to keep the house of cards from falling apart. For every \$12,000, eight people had to initially "lose" \$1,500. There was also the small matter of the fact that the FBI frowned upon the operation of a Ponzi scheme so this whole charade fell apart when law enforcement found out about it.[4]

I know what you're thinking.

THESE STORIES ARE INSANE!

A secret inheritance from a Nigerian prince?!

Handing over your life savings to a pyramid scheme because of good vibes?!

And these stories do sound insane when you're not personally involved. But people make insane decisions with their money all the time. You may never become involved in a Ponzi scheme or hand your money over to a 14-year-old kid from Africa posing as royalty, but everyone makes mistakes when it comes to their finances. We are emotional beings, and money tends to bring out the worst in those emotions.

The world is a complex place. No one has it all figured out. We want to believe there's an easy path to improve our finances, health, and relationships. A secret club that's reserved only for those lucky enough to stumble across the Holy Grail that will cure us of our ills. I wish that Holy Grail existed, but there is no tried and true way to get rich overnight or fix your life through the powerful words of a guru.

Most of the stories you read in this book will make you think, *"There's no way that could ever happen to me."* The truth is, even if you never fall prey to massive fraud or a Ponzi scheme, everyone makes dumb decisions with their money. It's in our DNA. Most business and finance books tell you how to be successful. They purport to give you the secret, the recipe, the motivational quote, or the simple steps to earn riches or emulate successful entrepreneurs, business models, investors, or CEOs. This is not one of those books. The problem with only studying successes is they're often overflowing with survivorship bias. You never hear about all of the other failed businesses, ideas, or individuals who tried a similar route but failed. The person who won the lottery can't teach you how to follow their path to success and riches.

There is much more to learn from failures, fraud, charlatans, shady sales practices, and scams because it gives you some idea of what to avoid. There is no formula for getting rich quickly. No top-ten list or morning routine of high-functioning CEOs will automatically make you a successful entrepreneur. But studying poor decisions, gullible individuals, hucksters, irrational human behavior, and mental errors can help you see these things in yourself. Avoiding stupidity is often more helpful than trying to emulate brilliance. Even brilliant people can make bad decisions (as you will learn throughout these chapters). Money is one of the most unifying mediums on the planet. People of all levels of wealth – the rich, the poor, and everyone in between – make dumb decisions with their money. The simple reason for this is because money decisions have nothing to do with finances and everything to do with human nature.

The goal of this book is to help you make better decisions by learning from the mistakes of others and avoid getting taken advantage of.

Notes

1. McKinley E. Nigerian prince scam took $110K from Kansas man; 10 years later, he's getting it back. The Kansas City Star [Internet]. 2018 Jun 11. Available from: https://www.kansascity.com/news/state/kansas/article212657689.html
2. Neuffer E. 'Airplane': high-stakes chain letter. The New York Times [Internet] 1987 Apr 7. Available from: https://www.nytimes.com/1987/04/07/nyregion/airplane-high-stakes-chain-letter.html
3. Ibid.
4. Enscoe D. Pyramid scheme takes off thousands invest in 'plane game'. South Florida Sun Sentinel [Internet]. 1987 Mar 26. Available from: https://www.sun-sentinel.com/news/fl-xpm-1987-03-26-8701190859-story.html

CHAPTER 1

No One Sells Miracles

It's not a lie if you believe it.

—George Costanza

In the late 1980s a group of chemists from Pfizer created a compound called sildenafil citrate. It was developed to fight cardiovascular diseases such as high blood pressure and chest pain. The project was called UK92480 (the UK is because the chemists were based in the United Kingdom) – but even though it sounds top secret, it ended up being a low drug on the totem pole because of disappointing test results. No one involved with the effort thought they were onto something groundbreaking at the time.[1]

In fact, in the summer of 1993, the group was given an ultimatum that unless they could come back in the fall with conclusive data, it was time to close up shop and move on. Just a few short days later the researchers were doing a study on a group of miners in South Wales. Per protocol, they asked the miners if they noticed anything different after taking the drug. One of the men spoke up and said, "Well, I seemed to have more erections during the night than normal." The other men grinned and nodded in agreement.[2] One of the nurses in another clinical trial around the same time also noticed many of the men were lying on their stomachs, embarrassed that they ended up with an erection after taking the drug. A drug that was meant to treat cardiovascular disease was having very surprising unintended consequences.[3]

One of the main causes of chest pain is a condition called angina, which has to do with a reduced flow of blood to the heart. The reason this chest pain occurs is because the vessels that supply your heart with blood become constricted, which leads to pain in your chest as well as shortness of breath. Scientists often know how certain compounds are supposed to work but they don't always know if they will have the intended effect on the intended area of the body. The idea behind sildenafil was that it would dilate the blood vessels in the heart, thus reducing chest pain and breathlessness. Instead, the blood vessels in the penis became dilated. This drug inhibited the enzyme that breaks down a chemical that is key to the biology behind an erection.[4]

This isn't the first time a drug was discovered by accident. After vacationing in Scotland for a month in 1928, a pathologist named Andrew Fleming returned to his laboratory to discover he had left a petri dish on a windowsill at a hospital in London. Fleming was growing bacteria in these dishes but noticed the one he accidentally left out had grown an airborne fungus. The fungus stopped the bacteria dead in its tracks. This mold was called Penicillium notatum. Fleming inadvertently made one of the most important discoveries in the history of medicine. He created the antibiotic penicillin.[5]

It can't be overstated how huge this discovery was. At the time, the average life span in the United States was under 60 years of age. That number is now around 80 years old, and Fleming's accidental discovery had a lot to do with this. Fleming would later say, "When I woke up just after dawn on 28 September, 1928, I certainly didn't plan to revolutionize all medicine by discovering the world's first antibiotic, or bacteria killer. But I suppose that was exactly what I did." [6]

A failed cardiovascular drug that gave men erections didn't have quite the same impact as penicillin, but these scientists did stumble across one of the most successful drugs of the modern era. Today we know of this drug as Viagra. According to Pfizer, since it was officially launched in 1998, 62 million men from around the globe have purchased the erectile dysfunction drug. It's estimated that people in the US alone spend almost $1.5 billion on Viagra each year. Even the US military is said to spend almost $42 million on the little blue pill.[7]

A few months after the drug was released, there were over 300,000 prescriptions filled in a single week. Obviously, there was a ton of pent-up demand for this product. Before Viagra's approval by the FDA in 1998, there really was no treatment for erectile dysfunction. The only options available included a painful injection or an implant, not exactly as easy as popping a little blue pill in your mouth. And before even penicillin was discovered, men went to far greater lengths to cure their libido.[8]

Goats as Viagra?

Before the discovery of penicillin the field of medicine was full of quacks, hucksters, and charlatans. The general public knew so little about their healthcare options that it was easy to take advantage of people's ignorance. In the early 1900s the entire field of medicine was still in its infancy in many ways. The American Medical Association was founded in 1847 but each state still had its own licensing board which led to a lax system of oversight and ease of corruption because no one knew any better. Medical quackery isn't exactly like the typical financial scams that go after our need for greed. Instead, it preys on our worst fears: mainly death, disease, and our hope that miracles do truly exist when it comes to healing.

Samuel Hopkins Adams wrote a series of articles in 1905 entitled "The Great American Fraud." He wrote, "Gullible America will spend some $75 million (that's more than $2.1 billion in today's dollars) in the purchase of patent medicines. In consideration of this sum it will swallow huge quantities of alcohol, an appalling amount of opiates and narcotics, a wide assortment of varied drugs ranging from powerful and dangerous heart depressants to insidious liver stimulants; and, far in excess of other ingredients, undiluted fraud."[9]

The wild west that was the medical profession was the perfect fit for Dr. John Brinkley. Brinkley never actually finished medical school, instead opting to purchase a diploma for $100 which granted him the ability to practice medicine in eight states. Unbelievably, this was all it took to practice medicine in the early twentieth century. Still in his 20s, Brinkley opened up a doctor's office in Greenville, South Carolina with a partner. They took out ads in the local paper which asked:

ARE YOU A MANLY MAN FULL OF VIGOR?

Each morning the two "doctors" would ask the patients who answered the ad different questions, take some notes, collect $25 – a massive sum at the time – and inject colored water into their posteriors.

They called the treatment electric medicine and claimed it came from Germany. The two men skipped town a few months later to avoid those who figured out their scam. After running out of money, Brinkley found a newspaper ad looking for a doctor in Kansas, in a town called Milford with a population of just 200 people. So he and his wife Minnie moved to Milford to open up a doctor's office and drugstore.[10]

The couple were barely making ends meet when a 46-year-old farmer named Bill Stittsworth came into their office. Stittsworth said he and his wife had been unsuccessfully trying to get pregnant for 16 years. "I'm a flat tire," he told the Brinkleys. Then Stittsworth looked out the window at a nearby farm and observed, "Too bad I don't have billy goat nuts." You see, billy goats are known to be some of the healthiest, most fertile animals on the planet. The farmer knew firsthand a goat's appetite for sex was famous.[11]

No one really knows exactly what happened next. Brinkley claims the farmer begged him to try an experimental procedure using goat glands. The farmer's family claims Brinkley paid Stittsworth to experiment on him. Regardless of whose idea it was, a few nights later both men were back in the office prepping for a unique surgical procedure. Brinkley slit the farmer's scrotum, after which he reached for two goat testicles that were sitting on a small silver tray, implanted a goat testis on each side of the scrotum, and sutured them to the loose tissue. Stittsworth had his man parts sewn up and the whole ordeal was over in 15 minutes.[12]

Two weeks later the farmer showed up and told Brinkley the good news – his wife was finally pregnant! They named their child Billy, after a goat, of course. The second couple who conceived a child after having the goat gland surgery named their child Charles Darwin Mellinger, in honor of science of all things. Brinkley unwittingly stumbled onto a genius marketing campaign for the rural population in a small Kansas town. The goat gland surgery became an instant hit. His operation became so personalized he would even let the patients select their own goat from his backyard. Brinkley was averaging 50 procedures a month in no time, at $750 a pop (a lot of money for the 1920s and around $9,000 in today's dollars). Eventually he began implanting goat ovaries in women as well, to double his clientele.[13]

Spoiler alert: Implanting goat testicles into men's scrotums is not a scientifically backed procedure. Most people didn't stop to think about how insane this was at the time because they were desperate. A few weeks after his first goat gland transplant, Brinkley told a classroom full of other doctors, "I have a scheme up my sleeve and the whole world will hear of it." The way he was going to get the whole world to hear about his plan was through a brand-new technology that would take his operation to the next level.

Radio

Radio was an entirely new medium for the mainstream public in the 1920s. It not only allowed broadcasters to reach large groups of people all at once across the country, it also allowed them to capture people's attention in their own homes. Radio was truly one of the first technological breakthroughs that allowed families to have leisure time with one another in their own living rooms where they didn't have to pay attention to one another.

Companies began advertising their products in the late nineteenth century, but the 1920s is when advertising exploded into popular culture. The radio had a great deal to do with its spread. The first commercial radio station was launched in 1920. By the end of the decade, radio penetration went from basically zero to close to 40% of households. By 1940, more than 80% of households had a radio. The adoption of radios in households was faster than electricity, automobiles, or the telephone. Comedian George Burns wrote in his biography, "It's impossible to explain the impact the radio had on the world to anyone who didn't live through that time."[14]

Radio sales doubled in 1923, and then tripled from there by 1924. The biggest reason radio spread like wildfire is because it was free. There was nothing else to pay for once you purchased it. And the reason it was free is because the business model was predicated on advertising. The swift rise in radio ownership coincided perfectly with Brinkley's rise to prominence as a healer of all things to all people with ailments. Brinkley was a world-class charlatan, but according to one media historian he was also, "the man who, perhaps, more than any other, foresaw the great potentialities of radio as an advertising medium."[15]

Advertising these days is everywhere you look. It's on the websites, social media, billboards, TV, radio, and podcasts. But advertising wasn't always so ingrained in our lives. When the radio went mainstream in the 1920s and revolutionized how we communicate with large groups of people, it was controversial to advertise on the platform. In 1922, future president Herbert Hoover even said, "It is inconceivable that we should allow so great a possibility for service, for news, for entertainment, for education, and for vital commercial purposes to be drowned out in advertising chatter."[16]

Brinkley saw the future well before many businesses and invested heavily into radio to spread his message. By 1923, tiny Milford, Kansas had the fourth largest radio station in the country. How did Brinkley pull off this feat? He was essentially the Dr. Ruth of his day, talking about sex on the radio, something that was a taboo subject at the time. He also used radio as a sales tactic for his services and the new line of "medicine" he created. The radio show he produced was basically the WebMD of the early twentieth century. People would write in questions about their illness or injury, which Brinkley would read aloud on his show. Prescriptions were then given on air, which listeners could then go buy from the more than 500 drugstores he developed relationships with all over the country.[17]

No self-respecting doctor would hand out prescriptions without first examining the patient and making a diagnosis, but Brinkley wasn't trying to appeal to reason: he was trying to appeal to people's worst fears. Snake oil salesmen had always targeted people's emotions, and Brinkley was no different. Now he had the ability to do so on a massive scale. This entailed not only promoting his goat gland operation, but an entire line-up of healthcare products and services.

The Kansas State Medical Board eventually revoked his medical license on the grounds of "gross immorality and unprofessional conduct." The Kansas City Star proclaimed: "The superquack of Milford is finished."[18]

Narrator: *He was not finished.*

The Placebo Effect

Morris Fishbein, an actual physician with morals who worked with the AMA, had made it his life's work to take down hucksters and quacks, and the man at the top of his list was John Brinkley. Fishbein knew Brinkley's ruse couldn't last forever. The goat gland procedure was completely fabricated. There wasn't an ounce of scientific or biological proof it could work.

The question you're probably asking yourself is this: How the hell did it actually work for those farmers who went through this painful procedure? It could have been due to the placebo effect, but the true answer is likely simple regression to the mean. Most sick people tend to get better. In fact, it's estimated that four out of every five physical ailments will heal themselves.[19] So even the biggest quack in the world could "heal" most patients through the passage of time or dumb luck. Unfortunately, it was those patients who came to Brinkley in dire need of treatment who suffered the most.

The Kansas Medical Board proved that at least 42 people Brinkley treated (some of whom were not sick before he treated them) had died after undergoing one of his operations or medicine programs. This number is significantly higher than almost any serial killer in history. At least six of those people had undergone the goat gland transplant. Not only was Brinkley performing medical procedures with no scientific reasoning behind them, but he would often treat patients while drunk. One patient claimed that instead of stitching him up after a prostate operation, Brinkley used a piece of rubber from a boot heel to patch him up.[20] The worst part about these statistics is they occurred at the midpoint of his career. He was far from completing his medical reign of terror.

Fishbein finally put together enough evidence to bring Brinkley to trial. It was during this trial that the prosecution used Brinkley's own autobiography against him. Consistent with his personality, Brinkley's autobiography was filled with lies and fabricated stories. Even though he never graduated from medical school, Brinkley gave the date of his graduation in the book. The prosecution pointed out Brinkley was actually in jail on that date. In his writings Brinkley compared himself to Martin Luther, Galileo, and Jesus Christ. The lies and deceit finally caught up with him. After practicing medicine in Texas and Mexico, even going so far as starting a radio show south of the border (since he was barred from broadcasting in the US), he was forced to declare bankruptcy in 1941. The malpractice lawsuits finally caught up with him and he died a year later.[21]

Correlation Does Not Imply Causation

People often have a difficult time understanding the idea that correlation does not imply causation. Just because women were getting pregnant after their husbands received goat testicle implants does not mean that's what caused them to bear children. The world is full of examples of two things that appear to be related because they move in concert with one another, merely by chance. The number of films actor Nicolas Cage appeared in is highly correlated with the number of people who drown in a swimming pool each year. The divorce rate in the state of Maine neatly tracks the annual consumption of margarine.[22]

There's an old saying that the data will tell you anything if you torture it long enough. Investor David Leinweber once ran a test to show how data can be manipulated. He found that the production of butter in Bangladesh could have been used to predict how well the US stock market would perform between 1983 and 1993. When butter production was up 1%, the S&P 500 would be up 2% the following year. And if butter production was down 10%, the S&P 500 would fall 20%. This relationship has no basis in reality but I'm guessing if you showed enough people the backtest, some of them would begin to believe they'd found a foolproof system to beat the stock market.[23]

Brinkley's client list was said to include former Secretary of State William Jennings Bryan and the 28th President of the United States, Woodrow Wilson. Actor Buster Keaton even mentioned Brinkley and the goat testicle transplant in one of his movies in the 1920s. A US Senator from Colorado named Wesley Staley went so far as to say, "I wear goat glands and am proud of it," in his public defense of Brinkley. A US Senator seriously said this out loud. To other people.[24]

Unfortunately, there will always be charismatic charlatans like Brinkley around to take advantage of human nature. Certain people have the ability to convince others they can make the impossible become routine. Brinkley became fabulously wealthy from his practice and it was a boon for the town of Milford. Brinkley paid for a new hospital and put in sidewalks, a new post office, and a sewage system. He even bought new uniforms for the Little League team, who were aptly named the Brinkley Goats.[25]

Not long after having his license revoked for practicing medicine in the state of Kansas, Brinkley decided to try his hand at politics by running for governor. The campaign was marked by all sorts of outlandish promises he couldn't possibly keep – every county would have its own lake, free books, and free healthcare for all. The campaign was ridiculous from the word go and somehow, he still almost won![26] Being active in charitable causes, politics, or the local community are all wonderful ways to get people off your scent when bilking unsuspecting victims in a financial scam.

Fear and greed lend a hand in every financial mishap, and Brinkley's tale is no different. The man himself was driven by greed and an inner desire to prove his critics wrong. It's estimated Brinkley was bringing in more than $1 million a year during the Great Depression. This was an astronomical sum back then but even more outlandish when you consider average wages across the country were dropping like a rock, falling around 40% in 1932 alone.[27] To satiate his greed, Brinkley preyed on the fears of other (mostly) men who were ashamed of their lack of sexual prowess, the sick and injured who were in search of a miracle, and the uneducated who didn't know any better and simply trusted someone who sounded like they knew what they were talking about. Even his wife Minnie was under his spell until the very end. She outlived her husband by nearly 40 years and claimed until her dying day that successful goat gland procedures were still being performed in secret all around the world.[28]

Same as It Ever Was

It's easy to look back now at how gullible people in the early twentieth century were when it came to the charms of quacks and snake oil salesmen. That is until you realize those same techniques still work today. Just think of all the scams available for those looking to lose weight, improve their finances, and hold on to their youth. The AMA spent years trying to discredit Brinkley, but he had the power of persuasion, a medium of communication to the masses, and a sales technique that would have allowed him to sell water to a whale.

Healthcare has improved by leaps and bounds since Brinkley began his reign of terror on the Midwest, but that doesn't mean there will always be a unique procedure to solve all your ills. The same is true in all facets of life. The world is a complicated, dynamic place that doesn't always lend itself to easy solutions. There's no recipe for creating a hit movie. Scouts still don't know what makes one quarterback better than another when selecting a top pick in the NFL draft. There's no secret formula to earn vast riches overnight in the stock market. And there's no blueprint entrepreneurs can follow to create the next Apple or Google.

There's a New Yorker cartoon that shows a billboard planted in a field of sheep with a picture of a wolf that reads, "I am going to eat you." One of the sheep says to another sheep, "He tells it like it is." Brinkley was the wolf in this analogy while his patients were the sheep. At Brinkley's funeral in 1942, an anonymous man in the crowd supposedly confessed, "I knowed [sic] he was bilking me, but…I liked him anyway."[29]

Miracles may in fact exist, but don't expect someone to sell them to you.

Notes

1. Tozzi J and Hopkins JS. The little blue pill: an oral history of Viagra. *Bloomberg* [Internet]. 2017 Dec 11. Available from: https://www .bloomberg.com/news/features/2017-12-11/the-little-blue-pill-an-oral-history-of-viagra
2. Ibid.
3. Foley KE. Out of the blue pill: Viagra's famously surprising origin story is actually a pretty common way to find new drugs. *Quartz* [Internet]. 2017 Sept 10. Available from: https://qz.com/1070732/viagras-famously-surprising-origin-story-is-actually-a-pretty-common-way-to-find-new-drugs/
4. Tozzi J and Hopkins JS. The little blue pill: an oral history of Viagra. *Bloomberg* [Internet]. 2017 Dec 11. Available from: https://www .bloomberg.com/news/features/2017-12-11/the-little-blue-pill-an-oral-history-of-viagra
5. Rudd J. From Viagra to Valium, the drugs that were discovered by accident. *The Guardian* [Internet]. 2017 Jul 11. Available from: https:// www.theguardian.com/lifeandstyle/2017/jul/11/from-viagra-to-valium-the-drugs-that-were-discovered-by-accident
6. Pinsker J. Why we live 40 years longer today than we did in 1880. *The Atlantic* [Internet]. 2013 Nov. Available from: https://www.theatlantic. com/magazine/archive/2013/11/die-another-day/309541/
7. Foley KE. Out of the blue pill: Viagra's famously surprising origin story is actually a pretty common way to find new drugs. *Quartz* [Internet]. 2017 Sept 10. Available from: https://qz.com/1070732/viagras-famously-surprising-origin-story-is-actually-a-pretty-common-way-to-find-new-drugs/
8. Naish J. Is Viagra a cure or a curse? As Britain is the first country to make it available over the counter, John Naish on the wonder sex drug. *Daily Mail* [Internet]. 2017 Dec 1. Available from: https://www.daily-mail.co.uk/health/article-5134761/A-cure-curse-JOHN-NAISH-wonder-sex-drug.html
9. Adams SH. *The Great American Fraud*. OTB ebook Publishing; 2016.
10. Brock P. Charlatan: *America's Most Dangerous Huckster, the Man Who Pursued Him, and the Age of Flimflam*. New York: Three Rivers Press; 2008.

11. Lane P. Nuts! [film]. 2016.
12. Brock P. Charlatan: *America's Most Dangerous Huckster, the Man Who Pursued Him, and the Age of Flimflam*. New York: Three Rivers Press; 2008.
13. Lane P. Nuts! [film]. 2016.
14. Gordon RJ. *The Rise and Fall of American Growth: The U.S. Standard of Living Since the Civil War. The Princeton Economic History of the Western World*. Princeton, New Jersey: Princeton University Press; 2016.
15. Brock P. Charlatan: *America's Most Dangerous Huckster, the Man Who Pursued Him, and the Age of Flimflam*. New York: Three Rivers Press; 2008.
16. Wu T. *The Attention Merchants: The Epic Scramble to Get Inside Our Heads*. New York: Knopf Doubleday Publishing Group; 2016.
17. Lane P. Nuts! [film]. 2016
18. Brock P. Charlatan: *America's Most Dangerous Huckster, the Man Who Pursued Him, and the Age of Flimflam*. New York: Three Rivers Press; 2008.
19. Alexander S. Powerless placebos. Slate Star Codex [Internet]. 2018 Jan 31. Available from: https://slatestarcodex.com/2018/01/31/powerless-placebos/?platform=hootsuite
20. Brock P. Charlatan: *America's Most Dangerous Huckster, the Man Who Pursued Him, and the Age of Flimflam*. New York: Three Rivers Press; 2008.
21. The case of Brinkley vs. Fishbein: proceedings of a libel suit based on an article published in Hygeia. Jama Network [Internet] 1939 May 13; 112(19):1952–68. Available from: https://jamanetwork.com/journals/jama/article-abstract/288277
22. Vigen T. Spurious correlations. [Internet]. Available from: http://www.tylervigen.com/spurious-correlations
23. Washington L. What's the stock market got to do with the production of butter in Bangladesh? CNN Money [Internet]. 1998 Mar 1. Available from: https://money.cnn.com/magazines/moneymag/moneymag_archive/1998/03/01/238606/index.htm
24. Kindley E. Nuts!: a questionable cure for impotence. *The New Republic* [Internet]. 2016 Jul 22. Available from: https://newrepublic.com/article/135422/nuts-questionable-cure-impotence
25. Brock P. Charlatan: *America's Most Dangerous Huckster, the Man Who Pursued Him, and the Age of Flimflam*. New York: Three Rivers Press; 2008.
26. Lane P. Nuts! [film]. 2016
27. Allen F. Since yesterday: The 1930s in America. New York: Open Road Media; 1931.
28. Brock P. Charlatan: *America's Most Dangerous Huckster, the Man Who Pursued Him, and the Age of Flimflam*. New York: Three Rivers Press; 2008.
29. Ibid.

CHAPTER 2

How to Sell Anything

There are some frauds so well conducted that it would be stupidity not to be deceived by them.

—Charles Cotton

The Eiffel Tower is one of the most recognizable and well-traf-ficked monuments in the world. Each year, it's estimated well over six million visitors wait in long lines to experience this gorgeous landmark. It may be hard to believe, but when it was built the tower was subject to ridicule and was only supposed to stand for 20 years before being disassembled.

Gustave Eiffel designed his namesake tower for the 1889 World's Fair in Paris. No one had ever built a structure so tall before so the fact that it was erected in just over two years is a technical feat that was unparalleled at the time. Naysayers told Eiffel the tower would be impossible to build. The wind would make it too dangerous for people to ascend to such heights and the government wasn't keen on spending an estimated $1 million on the project. His contract stipulated that the tower would be allowed to stand for 20 years to be able to earn enough of a profit to make it worthwhile, at which point the erector set–looking structure would be taken down piece by piece.

The engineering and construction involved required an incredible amount of precision. The iron plates used to build the tower would have stretched 43 miles long if they were laid end-to-end and called for over seven million holes to be drilled into them. The iron used to construct the tower weighed over 7,000 tons and required more than 60 tons of paint. Each piece was traced out to be accurate within a tenth of a millimeter. There were 2.5 million rivets used in construction. Including the flagpole at the top, the Eiffel Tower reached 1,000 feet in height when it was finished.[1]

Although the tower was more beautiful than most could have imagined, it was initially panned by critics. Many of France's leading artists and intellectuals derided the tower, calling it "a truly tragic street lamp" and an "iron gymnasium apparatus, incomplete, confused, and deformed." The Americans and Brits weren't fans either, mostly because they were jealous. The *New York Times* called it "an abomination and eyesore." Editors at the *London Times* referred to it as the "monstrous erection in the middle of the noble public buildings of Paris." Americans didn't appreciate how the Eiffel Tower surpassed the Washington Monument as the tallest man-made structure at that time. Once it was completed even the most ardent critics eventually came around to the fact that it was a masterpiece, yet the government still wasn't positive they would keep the structure in place forever. In the years after the tower was built it began to fall into disrepair. It was costing the city a fortune in maintenance and upkeep.[2]

A man by the name of Victor Lustig saw this situation as an opportunity to profit from the uncertainty surrounding the future of this magnificent monument. Lustig decided he would sell the Eiffel Tower to the highest bidder … twice.

The Count

The man who tried to sell the Eiffel Tower had up to 45 different aliases. No one knew his real name or exactly where he came from, but he told authorities at one point his name was Robert Miller. As a young man traveling on an ocean liner from Europe to America, Miller came up with the name Victor "the Count" Lustig to fit in with the aristocrats on the ship. The name was a ploy to gain their trust. An ability to know his audience and adapt to any situation would prove to be an invaluable asset to Lustig over time. He began his career as a gambler but graduated to financial scams after figuring out how the wealthy class operated.

The Count's most successful scam was called the Romanian Money Box. To find his marks, Lustig would hang around expensive hotels, arriving by limo to show he belonged with the upper echelon of society. In bars and restaurants he would casually let it slip that he owned a secret money-printing box. After the seed was planted, the mark would go to Lustig's hotel room for a demonstration of how the contraption worked. Lustig would insert a single $100 bill into a small slot in the machine, which was a small wooden box full of knobs and brass dials. A substance called "radium" was Lustig's secret weapon for copying the bills. At least that's what he told his unsuspecting victims. For show, he would turn a few knobs and tell the person the only downside was that it took six hours to make a new bill using this secret substance.

After dinner and drinks, they would head back up to the room to find that a perfect copy of the $100 bill had popped out the other end of the box. When the wealthy elite saw this magical money-making machine actually worked they would offer to buy it on the spot. But the Count played it cool, always holding out for a short time, which invariably drove up the price people were willing to pay.[3] One of the best ways to persuade someone to do something is to allow them to come to the conclusion themselves. Once you've convinced yourself you're going to do something, you are unlikely to change your mind. Lustig let them convince themselves it was worth it.

Of course, no such magical box that could produce perfect copies of $100 bills actually existed. The "copies" that came out of the box were actual $100 bills Lustig had placed in the jury-rigged machine himself. Blinded by their greed, people would pay tens of thousands of dollars for a machine that had just $200 in it. The beauty of his scam is it would take 12 hours to produce those two bills and by the time these people realized they'd been swindled, Lustig had half a day of a head start to make his exit.

After wearing out his welcome in New York City, Lustig decided to try his hand in Chicago. In the 1920s, Al Capone ran the criminal rackets in the Windy City. Lustig was fearless, so he decided to pay a visit to the notorious gangster when he got to town to seek Capone's approval to operate on the mob boss's territory. Lustig told Capone he needed $50,000 to pull off a grand trade, promising the mobster he could double his money in just two months. The man known as Scarface said, "Okay, Count, double it in 60 days like you said." Two months later he was back in front of Capone asking for forgiveness. The get-rich-quick scheme had fallen through. Capone was furious. Just as he was about to explode, Lustig handed the crime boss his original $50,000 investment back and said, "Here, sir, is your money, to the penny. Again, my sincerest apologies. This is most embarrassing. Things didn't work out the way I had thought they would, I should have loved to have doubled your money for you and for myself – Lord knows that I need it – but the plan just did not materialize."[4]

Capone told Lustig he was expecting either $100,000 or nothing so he was taken aback by the man's honesty. Somehow the most notorious gangster on the planet not only gave him a pass, but Capone even counted out $5,000 from the pile to give the Count a head start in his business dealings! Here's the kicker: Lustig had never even dreamed up a money scheme to begin with. The $50,000 was sitting in a security box the entire month. It was his plan all along to gain the mob boss's trust and that's exactly what he did. Of course, Lustig was only playing an honest man for this ruse. He once said, "I cannot stand honest men. They lead desperate lives, full of boredom."[5]

Selling the Eiffel Tower

After a number of run-ins with the law, Lustig was looking to pull off one last big score to get out of the life of a con artist. Because the authorities in the US were onto his hijinks, Lustig went to Paris to pull off his pièce de résistance. Around the time Lustig returned to Paris, there were many stories in the local papers about the dilapidated state of the famous Eiffel Tower. A lightbulb went off in Lustig's head. He set about creating a fake government role for himself, complete with his own stationary and business cards done up with an official French seal. There was even an official-sounding, yet completely made-up title: "Deputy Director General of the Ministry of Posts and Telegraphs." Again using one of the finest hotels in the city, he set up shop at the Hôtel de Crillon, a stone palace on the Place de la Concorde. The biggest scrap metal dealers in town were summoned to the luxurious hotel for a secret business proposal.

"Because of engineering faults, costly repairs, and political problems I cannot discuss, the tearing down of the Eiffel Tower has become mandatory," he reportedly told this group in a quiet hotel room. The Count then shocked the small group of metal dealers by announcing the Eiffel Tower would be sold to the highest bidder. Many at the table were in disbelief but Lustig assured them if the government was able to turn a profit on the deal, it would minimize the protests from citizens.[6] The 1,000-foot tall structure contains more than 7,000 metric tons of iron, along with 2.5 million rivets that held it together, so these scrap metal dealers could calculate the sale of this amount of metal would net a fortune to those who tore it down and sold off the parts. To make the process more believable, the dealers were even taken on a tour of the monument to give them a better sense of the scale of the operation.

Bids were due by the next morning along with the promise of complete secrecy from those involved. Lustig told his marks the government didn't want word to get out for fear of a public outcry against tearing it down. Although he took bids from all interested parties, the patsy was picked out well in advance. Andre Poisson was relatively new to the area and trying to make a name for himself. What better way to make a name for yourself than by winning the biggest scrap metal project in the country's history? A few days later Lustig informed Poisson his offer of 250,000 francs (roughly $1 million today) was in fact the winning bid. Once he learned he won, Poisson finally became wary of the whole operation. So to seal the deal, Lustig demanded a bribe for securing the transaction. Everyone assumed all Parisian government officials were corrupt, so the bribe was the final nail in the coffin to make it seem legit. Poisson was in.[7]

Lustig secured the cash and handed over the "official" paperwork to finalize the sale. After a number of failed attempts to claim possession of the Eiffel Tower, Poisson finally realized he'd been swindled. By this point, Lustig had already fled the country. But a funny thing happened as he waited to see a news story about the man who tried to sell the Eiffel Tower – the story never came. Lustig was initially befuddled, but eventually realized Poisson was so embarrassed he was taken advantage of that he never bothered telling the authorities to save face. Never one to rest on his laurels, Lustig decided to test his good fortune by going back to Paris to try selling the Eiffel Tower a *second* time! This time he wasn't quite so lucky. The potential buyer went to the police before handing over the money, and Lustig was forced to flee the country yet again.[8]

Back in the States, the Count perfected his counterfeiting skills to the tune of more than $2.3 million over a five-year period. When the police finally apprehended him, Lustig had one more trick up his sleeve. As he awaited sentencing he pulled a jailbreak fit for a scene right out of a movie. Using a pair of stolen wire cutters (no one knows how he came to possess them) to open up his third-story window, he tied nine bedsheets together and used them as a rope to climb down three stories. The only problem was there was a crowd of roughly 100 people on Eleventh Avenue in New York City who saw him climbing down. Once he realized people were onto him, he took a rag from his pocket and pretended to clean the windows on his way down to pass himself off as a window cleaner. When he planted his feet on the ground, he gave the crowd a bow and ran away.[9]

Once the authorities finally caught up with the notorious con man, they took no chances, sending their new prisoner off to Alcatraz for a 20-year sentence. His death certificate listed his name as Robert V. Miller, but to this day no one knows his true identity or where he really came from. It wasn't until 1906 that Parisian officials extended the Eiffel Tower's contract to 1915, and a number of years later that they finally made it a permanent piece of the city's magnificent landscape.[10]

Everyone Is in Sales

In the movie *Gladiator*, Russell Crowe's character Maximus seeks the counsel of Proximo, a former champion gladiator, on how to win in the arena:

Maximus: You ask me what I want. I too want to stand before the Emperor as you did.

Proximo: Then listen to me. Learn from me. I wasn't the best because I killed quickly. I was the best because the crowd loved me. Win the crowd. And you will win your freedom.

Maximus: I will win the crowd. I will give them something they have never seen before.

Maximus did just that, shouting the best line of the movie to the crowd after one of his victories:

ARE YOU NOT ENTERTAINED?!

Maximus was a strong fighter and intelligent strategist but needed to sell himself to succeed. Lustig was one of the greatest con men ever because he knew how to win a crowd through some tried-and-true sales tactics. The actual product or service involved in his scams didn't matter all that much because Lustig was selling a dream, an easy way out, or an opportunity to get rich quickly. In a way, he was also an entertainer, giving the people what they wanted because he understood his marks so well. Even though his sole goal in life was to con others out of their money, there are some lessons we can learn from how Lustig approached the sales process.

Those in the sales profession get a bad rap in that most buyers assume salespeople are always trying to rip them off. But most things in life have an element of sales involved. Finding a good job is about selling yourself and your strengths. Finding a spouse is about marketing your good qualities. To put forward the thoughts and ideas that you care about requires the ability to convince others your opinions matter. This is especially true when you're first coming up in the working world without the requisite experience. Networking plays a huge role when finding a job these days, so you need the ability to convince others they should make a sale on your behalf to help with job opportunities.

Here are some of the most important aspects of the sales process to remember:

- **Know your audience.** When Spike Lee was making *Malcolm X* he knew the movie would go over budget before they even began shooting. The studio didn't have a budget for a three-hour movie but that's what Lee wanted. Out of that same budget, Lee was being paid $1 million to direct the film so he decided to put that entire amount right back into the movie, but it still wasn't enough. To get the movie made to his liking, Lee knew he needed to call up prominent people in the entertainment and professional sports worlds to get the remainder of the money. This would allow them to shoot a pivotal scene in South Africa as opposed to recreating South Africa on the Jersey Shore.

  Lee was able to secure money from the likes of Oprah, Prince, Tracy Chapman, and Janet Jackson. The last call he made was to Michael Jordan, arguably the greatest basketball player to ever play the game. But Lee went to Jordan's rival Magic Johnson first. Johnson asked how much he needed, Lee told him, and Magic immediately sent the money. Knowing Jordan was one of the most competitive people on the planet Lee admitted, "I just happened to let slip how much Magic wrote on his check," to which Jordan replied, "Magic gave how much?!" Not to be outdone, Jordan gave even more than Magic to seal the deal so the movie would be done to Lee's liking.[11]

If you want to get people to act, you first have to understand your audience.

- **Everyone can be sold to.** Leonardo da Vinci's *Salvador Mundi*, a 500-year-old painting of Jesus Christ, was rediscovered in 2007 at a regional auction where the original painting was masquerading as a copy.[12] Da Vinci's masterpiece was sold for a record-breaking $450.3 million in November 2017. Christie's handled the auction for the painting. To drum up interest they staged high-profile public exhibitions of the painting around the globe and created a video that was more or less an ad for the painting.[13] This confused some people at the time because the market for buyers of a painting that could sell for nearly half a billion dollars is quite small.

  The sales staff at Christie's personally knew the list of potential buyers because it was such an exclusive club. By making a show of the process and planting the seed that it was an iconic painting, they got this small billionaires club to value the painting more highly based on the premise that it must be more valuable if others consider it valuable. You may roll your eyes at the actions of people with more money than they know what to do with by "wasting" it on art, but this is simply human nature in action. We perceive value to be higher when others perceive value to be high. It's a vicious cycle but that's how all of this works in some ways.

- **Understand who has the informational advantage.** In the predigital days the seller had an enormous information advantage over the buyer. The Internet has leveled this playing field. People can actually look stuff up now and instantaneously compare products, services, and prices on their little handheld supercomputers. Everyone is in sales, whether they're selling products, services, or ideas. The trick is to find a way to do it without resorting to shady sales tactics that may have worked in the past. In his book, *The Win without Pitching Manifesto*, Blair Enns give three ways to sell for those who don't simply want to trick an unwitting customer:

  1. Help the unaware
  2. Inspire the interested
  3. Reassure those who have formed intent

Enns writes:

> The psychology of buying is the psychology of changing. Selling, therefore, is change management. The very best salespeople are respectful, selective facilitators of change. They help people move forward to solve their problems and capitalize on their opportunities. The rest talk people into things.[14]

Obviously, Victor Lustig talked people into things because he was a master manipulator with a huge ego. But he also understood people and utilized the soft skills of trust and persuasion as well as anyone. Never one to be shy from his own accomplishments, Lustig even penned a list called the Ten Commandments of the Con. Numbers three and four on the list show how eager he was to get in the good graces of his marks:

> Wait for the other person to reveal any political opinions, then agree with them.
> Let the other person reveal religious views, then have the same ones.

Trust is a huge component of the sales process because we prefer doing business with likeable, trustworthy people. When our ancestors were in small tribes and villages, the people around us were those we trusted the most, so our brains are hardwired to be more comfortable with people who seem trustworthy. Unfortunately, this is a double-edged sword as the people who often seem the most trustworthy are also the ones who possess the ability to take advantage of you. Trust, but verify.

Notes

1. Origins and construction of the Eiffel Tower. The official website of the Eiffel Tower [Internet]. Available from: https://www.toureiffel.paris/en/the-monument/history
2. Jonnes J. *Eiffel's Tower: The Thrilling Story Behind Paris's Beloved Monument and the Extraordinary World's Fair That Introduced It.* New York: Penguin Books; 2009.
3. Pizzoli G. *Tricky Vic: The Impossibly True Story of the Man Who Sold the Eiffel Tower.* New York: Penguin Group; 2015.
4. Nash JR. *Hustlers and Con Men: An Anecdotal History of the Confidence Man and His Games.* New York: M. Evans & Company, Inc.; 1976.

5. The day Al Capone was played for a sucker. *Chicago Tribune* [Internet]. 1976 Oct 5. Available from: https://chicagotribune.newspapers.com/image/383999447/?terms=victor%2Blustig%2Bcapone

6. Maysh J. The man who sold the Eiffel Tower. Twice. Smithsonian.com [Internet] 2016 Mar 9. Available from: https://www.smithsonianmag.com/history/man-who-sold-eiffel-tower-twice-180958370/

7. Velinger J. Victor Lustig – the man who (could have) sold the world. Radio Praha [Internet] 2003 Oct 15. Available from: https://www.radio.cz/en/section/czechs/victor-lustig-the-man-who-could-have-sold-the-world

8. Pizzoli G. *Tricky Vic: The Impossibly True Story of the Man Who Sold the Eiffel Tower.* New York: Penguin Group; 2015.

9. 'The Count' escapes jail on sheet rope. *The New York Times* [Internet]. 1935 Sep 2. Available from: https://timesmachine.nytimes.com/timesmachine/1935/09/02/93774752.pdf

10. Lustig sentenced to twenty-year term. *The New York Times.* [Internet]. 1935 Dec 10. Available from: https://timesmachine.nytimes.com/timesmachine/1935/12/10/93510100.html?pageNumber=30

11. Simmons B. The big Spike Lee sit-down, plus NBA trade value 2.0. The Bill Simmons Podcast Episode 479 [Internet]. 2019 Feb 6. Available from: https://www.theringer.com/the-bill-simmons-podcast/2019/2/6/18213368/bill-simmons-interviews-spike-lee-black-kklansman-knicks-porzingis-nba-trade-value

12. Leslie I. The death of Don Draper. The New Statesman [Internet]. 2018 Jul 25. Available from: https://www.newstatesman.com/science-tech/internet/2018/07/death-don-draper?amp

13. Crow K. $450 million! Record price for Leonardo da Vinci's 'Salvator Mundi' painting. Market Watch [Internet] 2017 Nov 16. Available from: https://www.marketwatch.com/story/450-million-record-price-for-leonardo-da-vincis-salvator-mundi-painting-2017-11-15

14. Enns B. *The Win Without Pitching Manifesto.* Nashville, Tennessee: Rock-Bench Publishing Corp; 2010.

CHAPTER 3

Fast Money

Comparison is the thief of joy.

—Teddy Roosevelt

Every year, Americans spend more money on the lottery than they do on movie tickets, music, professional sporting events, video games, and books combined.[1] According to a Gallup poll, more than half of American adults play the lottery in a given year.[2] There are numerous behavioral and psychological reasons people play the lottery despite such poor odds of ever winning. Near misses and actual successes activate the exact same region in the brain, so people who get a few numbers right here and there keep playing because they were *so close.*[3]

Our brains have a difficult time dealing with large numbers. People have a hard time comprehending the difference between, say, odds of 1 out of 2,000 versus odds of 1 out of 300,000,000.

The odds are astronomically low that you'll ever win the jackpot but it's always fun to dream about what you would do with oodles of found money. Maybe you would do some good with your winnings. Pay off your debts. Buy a new house. Help those in need. Go on your dream vacation. But there's also a high likelihood you would blow through the money. Research shows people who win $50,000 to $150,000 in the lottery are actually more likely than the average American to declare bankruptcy within three to five years.[4] And lottery winners rarely save much of their winnings. One study found lottery winners saved just 16 cents for every dollar they won.[5] A 16% savings rate is better than most Americans, but this also means 84 cents on the dollar from these winnings were spent.

There are countless stories of people who won big only to blow it all. William "Bud" Post won more than $16 million in 1988 by playing the lottery. It didn't help him as much as one would think. Post lost about a third of it to one of his former wives who sued him for her portion of the winnings. Then his own brother hired a hit man to kill him for his money. Luckily, the attempted assassination never got off the ground. Unfortunately, Post was forced to file for bankruptcy within a year of winning after legal bills and out-of-control spending habits wrecked his windfall. He lived on Social Security and food stamps until he died broke in 2006. Post said of winning the lottery, "I wish it never happened. It was totally a nightmare. I was much happier when I was broke."[6]

According to the Certified Financial Planner Board of Standards, almost one-third of lottery winners declare bankruptcy. These winners ended up in a worse place than they were in before winning gobs of money. Lottery winners have also been shown to be more susceptible to drug and alcohol abuse, depression, divorce, suicide, or estrangement from their family.[7]

Even the neighbors of lottery winners are more likely to go bankrupt than the average household. Researchers at the Federal Reserve discovered close neighbors of lottery winners in Canada were more likely to increase their spending, take on more debt, put more money into speculative investments, and eventually file for bankruptcy. And the larger the winnings, the more likely it was others in that neighborhood would go bankrupt.[8]

There's a lot to unpack here, but one of the main problems with fast money is you don't have time to acclimate to your newfound wealth. Most people spend their whole lives slowly building up their nest egg by saving methodically and growing their paycheck over time. This gives people time to adjust as income and wealth slowly build. People who come into large amounts of money very quickly don't have that same adjustment period. So while it can be fun to dream about, not everyone can handle the newfound responsibilities that come with fast money.

Wealth is simply the difference between what you make and what you spend, so the secret sauce to building wealth over time is avoiding lifestyle creep as your income rises. This is one of the reasons so many lottery winners go broke. Their lifestyle grows exponentially larger than their pile of money. It's also one of the main reasons so many professional athletes run into money problems. And when you make a ton of money, especially at a young age, there are bound to be vultures from the financial industry who are circling to take advantage of that newfound wealth. Enter Kirk Wright.

The Promise of Huge Returns with Minimal Effort

The median NFL player earns roughly $3.2 million over the course of their career, which lasts roughly 3.3 years on average. This is more money than most people earn in their entire lives but it's not always enough to see these players through their days after they hang up their pads. Unfortunately, almost 1 in 5 professional football players files for bankruptcy within 12 years of exiting the league. And many of those bankruptcies occur soon after retirement.

A group of economists gathered data on over 2,000 players drafted between 1996 and 2003, tracking earnings and bankruptcy filings of those players. Players start going broke two years or so after retiring through a combination of exorbitant spending, a lack of savings, and highly leveraged investments that go bad. These numbers were not impacted by the level of earnings or length of time playing, either. The authors of the study claimed, "Moreover, bankruptcy rates are not affected by a player's total earnings or career length. Having played for a long time and been well-paid does not provide much protection against the risk of going bankrupt."[9]

Steve Atwater was hoping he wouldn't fall into the same trap as those who blew through their millions in earnings. Atwater was an eight-time Pro Bowler and a two-time Super Bowl Champion with the NFL's Denver Broncos. At the University of Arkansas, Atwater majored in banking and finance while playing college ball. Following more than a decade playing professional football, he tried his hand at the stock market during his initial retirement years but eventually decided to outsource his investments to a professional.[10]

Atwater was the victim of financial fraud at one point, courtesy of Donald Lukens, an advisor who sold real estate investments. Lukens duped Atwater and 200 or so other investors by inflating property values, taking obscene commissions, lying about certain projects, and making the occasional transfer of funds from one investor to another to keep up his charade. Atwater lost a decent chunk of change, but he at least ended up owning a property outright as a consolation prize. With his next investment opportunity, he wouldn't be so lucky.[11]

Around the same time Atwater was seeking investment counsel, a wealth management firm in Atlanta was about to pique the interest of plenty of current and former NFL players.

In 2003, Kirk Wright's wealth management firm International Management Associates (IMA) earned a coveted spot on the NFL Players Association (NFLPA) Registered Financial Advisors Program. This preapproved list from the NFLPA gave Wright's firm access to some of the highest paid professional athletes in the world. Simply being included on this list gave an added element of trust in a business where trust is everything.

Wright's firm was added to the program in response to the Tarik Black scandal from the year before. Black was a former player turned money manager who was convicted of defrauding NFL players out of $12 million. Before the league began providing the players with a list of approved financial advisors, the NFLPA discovered in a study that 78 players were scammed out of $42 million over a period from 1999 to 2002.[12] IMA would make this fraud look like chump change by the time Wright was done bilking former players and other investors out of their money.[13]

Wright began his money management career on a small scale, pooling money with classmates while earning his master's degree at Harvard. After finishing school he mainly ran money for friends and family. The business grew once he formed a partnership with two anesthesiologists who had connections to wealthy friends and acquaintances in the southwest. Hundreds of well-off clients signed up to invest with Wright. IMA was off and running.[14]

Wright was polished, well-spoken, and had a knack for telling investors exactly what they wanted to hear. He hosted clients and prospects at seminars, hospitality suites during Atlanta Falcons' games, and private parties at his mansion. The pitch to investors was quite simple: they could earn huge returns with minimal risk and little effort. Who wouldn't want easy profits with little volatility in their investments? IMA's preferred method of investing was short-selling, a strategy that involves betting stocks will fall in value by borrowing shares, immediately selling them for cash, and hoping to buy back in at a lower price in the future to earn a profit on the difference.[15]

IMA's promotional materials were vague, but investors didn't seem to care all that much because the promoted returns were so juicy. Wright claimed annual returns of 20-25%. One of the funds, named the House Account, was said to give investors 10% returns *per month*! Most professional investors would kill to average 10% per year.[16] Ten percent a month is otherworldly, equating to more than 213% a year! And the presentation materials made these returns sound like they were a foregone conclusion.

John Pierpont (JP) Morgan is attributed with the quotation, "Nothing so undermines your financial judgement as the sight of your neighbor getting rich." This is truer among the wealthy class than any other group, because people with lots of money can be even more insecure than most when it comes to their station in life. There is always someone richer than you, even when you have a lot of money. You would assume rich people perform their own due diligence when it comes to making big money decisions, but word of mouth, jealousy, and envy often trump sound investment policy. Business executives, retirees, physicians, and professional athletes were all being told IMA was the place where rich people go to become *really* rich. They all wanted in, no questions asked.

The gains promised in the presentation materials never transpired for the simple fact that Wright was both a terrible investor and an outright fraud. Promoted trades were either money losers or made up so all of the money that supported his luxurious lifestyle came from new investors in the fund. It's easy to spend money when it's not yours, so Wright bought a $200,000 Lamborghini, threw a huge bash for his wedding reception good for half a million dollars, and remodeled his home to the tune of $1 million in upgrades.

The two Atlanta-area anesthesiologists who invested with IMA eventually became suspicious when Wright and his team cut off communication and stopped answering emails. They sued, which meant the SEC stepped in by bringing a suit against Wright and shutting down the operation in early 2006. Almost all of the $150 to $185 million in client money was unrecoverable. It was just ... gone.[17] When the authorities finally caught up with Wright, he was at a Ritz Carlton in Miami. Apparently, he had already registered for a new business in North Carolina, inevitably to scam even more people out of their money.[18]

Atwater handed over money from his savings, retirement accounts, and even his children's trust funds when he invested with
IMA. There were six other former NFL players, mostly Atwater's
friends, who were named in the suit against Wright. Atwater admitted after the fraud came to light, "I brought in my best friends. That
hurts more than my loss." Wright even took money from his own
mother for the scheme. After regulators poured through the actual
trades he made, it was discovered Wright had lost money on literally
every single real trade he ever made while shorting stocks. There
were no books or financial records to speak of for the company.
There were no tax returns. The only thing they could find was a
separate line item called the Expense Account. Wright would move
investor dollars into that account and then write checks for his own
lavish lifestyle.[19]

After being found guilty of four counts of fraud and larceny,
Wright took his own life in prison. The FBI found just $28,000 in
cash from an estimated $150 to $185 million in capital from around
500 clients. They were able to sell some of his assets and real estate,
but most clients lost nearly all of the money they handed over to
Wright. Trading losses added up to almost $31 million while the rest
was lost in other investments or personal spending.[20] Wright might
go down as one of the worst investors of all time.

When Trust Goes too Far

People trusted Wright because they trusted their friends, teammates,
and colleagues who recommended his services. Becoming wealthy
doesn't excuse you from paying attention to your finances. If anything, people with money need to be more attentive to the management of their wealth because rich people are constantly targeted by
hucksters, scam artists, and crooks. William Bernstein once wrote,
"The wealthy *are* different than you and I: they have more ways of
having their wealth stripped away." You can outsource expertise but
never your understanding, especially when it comes to your finances.
There are countless examples of people who were scammed out of
their money because they failed to do their homework.

NBA hall of famer and TV star Charles Barkley invested $6.1 million
with a man named Donald Watkins. Barkley sent the money to Watkins
without even running it by his financial advisor of many years, Glenn
Guthrie. Guthrie never got the chance to look over the terms of the

agreement or vet the investment documents. "That's the way Charles operated for lack of a better way to put it," Guthrie said. "When [Barkley] trusts somebody, he puts all [trust] in." According to Guthrie, Barkley said "This is mine and this is my investment. I want to do it."[21]

Barkley never saw that money again. It turns out Watkins committed bank fraud and conspiracy, of which he was eventually convicted in a court of law. Watkins fooled investors into believing he was a secret billionaire, which he was certainly not. In fact, Watkins struggled with credit card debt, back taxes, and overdrawn bank accounts. To make up for a shortfall in cash, he duped professional athletes, banks, friends, and even a girlfriend out of their money. Watkins claimed he was busy creating an eco-friendly waste disposal company, called Masada. The company never came to be, but he didn't let the facts get in the way of a good investment pitch to investors, including former NFL and NBA players.

Watkins even told two former NFL players "I'll take a f—ing before I let a friend get a f—ing because friendship is more valuable than money. Always has been. Always will be. You remember that." This was a lie. The money was never used to finance Masada, nor was it intended to. The company was never even his to begin with.[22]

In any service-related business, there will always be a huge element of trust involved because services are inherently an intangible good. It's a promise for the future, especially in the financial services industry. But that doesn't mean you can ever blindly take advice from someone simply because they come off as trustworthy. You still have to perform your due diligence, understand exactly what you're getting into, and know what you own and why you own it when making any investment decision. There are far more good salespeople in the world than worthwhile investment opportunities. Think and act accordingly.

Do Your Homework

Jim Chanos is likely the most well-known and successful short-seller of all time. Chanos founded Kynikos Capital Partners in 1985 and famously shorted Enron before it filed for bankruptcy in 2001. But his short investments, as represented by his long-standing short fund called Ursus, have lost just under 1% a year in that time.[23] Kynikos has another fund, their flagship offering, which uses leverage to go long stocks with 190% of capital and short 90% of the fund. The idea is by protecting the downside with short sales you can take more risk to the upside with your longs. Don't try this at home kids but it's obviously worked for Chanos as this fund has reportedly doubled up the return on the S&P 500 since inception.

But it's worth noting that one of the greatest short-sellers of all time didn't consistently make money shorting stocks. It was more of a risk management tool as opposed to a way to get rich for the simple fact that the market generally goes up over the long term. Shorting stocks may sound like a lucrative strategy until you actually do some digging and realize how hard it is to pick the losers in the face of a market that mostly rises over time.

Making money in the markets is never going to be easy, and anyone who tells you it is will be is fooling themselves (or most likely, you). But this game becomes harder still when you don't put in the time and effort necessary to understand how your money is being managed on your behalf. Wright claimed he had a secret recipe for stock market success but he never actually shared that secret with investors. This is what we call a red flag in the investment business.

Many assume professional athletes don't know what they're doing with their money. After all, they earn more money by the time they're 25-years-old than most people could dream about seeing in a lifetime. Yet this fraud wasn't just made up of professional football players. There were also many doctors, physicians and bright business people who handed over their money. Making a lot of money in the past can be one of the worst things that can happen to someone who wants to make money in the future. This is because we become overconfident in our abilities and attribute success to our own skills and failure to bad luck.

Jim Paul was a young futures trader in the pits of the Chicago Mercantile Exchange back when there were people screaming orders at each other while wearing those funny coats (think *Trading Places* with Eddie Murphy and Dan Aykroyd). Paul made a sizable amount of money at a young age and subsequently lost it all because he became overconfident. Paul later recalled the episode in his book, *What I Learned Losing a Million Dollars*, where he explained:

> Personalizing successes sets people up for disastrous failure. They begin to treat the success as a personal reflection rather than the result of capitalizing on a good opportunity, being at the right place at the right time or even being just plain lucky.

Personalizing successes can also open people up to being taken advantage of because wealthy people begin to feel invincible. Anthony Pratkanis, a psychology professor at the University of California, Santa Cruz gave an eight-question test to one group of people who were victims of financial fraud and another that wasn't. These weren't just basic questions but difficult queries that tested these people's knowledge of investments and the markets. The average score among victims of fraud was 58%. Not a perfect score, but non-victims of fraud got just two out of eight questions correct on average. So the people who were victims of fraud were actually more informed about investments than those who weren't. Pratkanis concluded, "Everyone gets taken. But it's the most sophisticated ones who are taken the most."[24]

Professional athletes and lottery winners definitely have a target on their backs when it comes to predatory behaviors by financial scam artists. This is true of anyone with money. Hucksters and snake oil salesmen don't discriminate among the wealthy class. If you have money, you must be aware of who you work with, what you'll invest in, and any particular blind spots you may have when making important money decisions. No one is going to care about your money more than you.

Notes

1. Isidore C. Americans spend more money on the lottery than on ... CNN Business [Internet]. 2015 Feb 11. Available from: https://money.cnn.com/2015/02/11/news/companies/lottery-spending/
2. Auter Z. About half of Americans play state lotteries. Gallup [Internet] 2016 Jul 22. Available from: https://news.gallup.com/poll/193874/half-americans-play-state-lotteries.aspx
3. Clark L, Lawrence AJ, Astley-Jones F, and Gray N. Gambling near-misses enhance motivation to gamble and recruit win-related brain circuitry. *Neuron.* 2009 Feb 12;61(3):481–90. doi: 10.1016/j.neuron.2008.12.031
4. Hankins S, Hoekstra M, and Skiba PM. The ticket to easy street? The financial consequences of winning the lottery. *The Review of Economics and Statistics.* 2011 Jul 21;93(3):961–969. doi: https://doi.org/10.1162/REST_a_00114
5. Imbens GW, Rubin DB, and Sacerdote BI. Estimating the effect of unearned income on labor earnings, savings, and consumption: evidence from a survey of lottery players. *American Economic Review.* 2001 Sep;91(4):778–94. doi: 10.1257/aer.91.4.778

6. Sullivan P. William 'Bud' Post III; unhappy lottery winner. *The Washington Post* [Internet]. 2006 Jan 20. Available from: http://www.washingtonpost.com/wp-dyn/content/article/2006/01/19/AR2006011903124.html

7. Edelman R. Why so many lottery winners go broke. *Fortune* [Internet]. 2016 Jan 15. Available from: http://fortune.com/2016/01/15/powerball-lottery-winners/

8. Agarwal S, Mikhed W, and Scholnick B. Does the relative income of peers cause financial distress? Evidence from lottery winners and neighboring bankruptcies. Federal Reserve Bank of Philadelphia WP18-16. 2018 May. doi: https://doi.org/10.21799/frbp.wp.2018.16

9. Carlson K, Kim J, Lusardi A, and Camerer CF. Bankruptcy rates among NFL players with short-lived income spikes. *American Economic Review*, American Economic Association. 2015 May;105(5):381–4. 10.3386/w21085

10. Fennessy S. The Wright stuff. *Atlanta* magazine [Internet] 2006 Oct. Available from: https://books.google.com/books?id=rQ8AAAAAMBAJ&pg=PA142&lpg=PA142&dq=kirk+wright+nfl&source=bl&ots=yZ-lenBxlV&sig=ACfU3U1uQBuJzeJ2fTAnfr3sp58qO4bhmw&hl=en&sa=X&ved=2ahUKEwjkttW63bvgAhVOOKwKHZFCATs4ChDoATAIegQIARAB#v=onepage&q=kirk%20wright%20nfl&f=false

11. Ibid.

12. Tierney M. Hedge fund manager's death does not halt suit against N.F.L. and players union. *The New York Times* [Internet]. 2008 Jun 2. Available from: https://www.nytimes.com/2008/06/02/sports/football/02wright.html

13. Fennessy S. The Wright stuff. *Atlanta* magazine [Internet] 2006 Oct. Available from: https://books.google.com/books?id=rQ8AAAAAMBAJ&pg=PA142&lpg=PA142&dq=kirk+wright+nfl&source=bl&ots=yZ-lenBxlV&sig=ACfU3U1uQBuJzeJ2fTAnfr3sp58qO4bhmw&hl=en&sa=X&ved=2ahUKEwjkttW63bvgAhVOOKwKHZFCATs4ChDoATAIegQIARAB#v=onepage&q=kirk%20wright%20nfl&f=false

14. Tierney M. Hedge fund manager's death does not halt suit against N.F.L. and players union. *The New York Times* [Internet]. 2008 Jun 2. Available from: https://www.nytimes.com/2008/06/02/sports/football/02wright.html

15. Horowitz C. Circuit court sides with NFL, players union in fraud suit. National Legal and Policy Center [Internet]. 2011 Mar 1. Available from: http://nlpc.org/2011/03/01/circuit-court-sides-nfl-players-union-fraud-suit/

16. Fennessy S. The Wright stuff. *Atlanta* magazine [Internet] 2006 Oct. Available from: https://books.google.com/books?id=rQ8AAAAAMBAJ&pg=PA142&lpg=PA142&dq=kirk+wright+nfl&source=bl&ots=yZ-len

BxlV&sig=ACfU3U1uQBuJzeJ2fTAnfr3sp58qO4bhmw&hl=en&sa=X&
ved=2ahUKEwjkttW63bvgAhVOOKwKHZFCATs4ChDoATAIegQIARA
B#v=onepage&q=kirk%20wright%20nfl&f=false

17. Horowitz C. Circuit court sides with NFL, players union in fraud suit. National Legal and Policy Center [Internet]. 2011 Mar 1. Available from: http://nlpc.org/2011/03/01/circuit-court-sides-nfl-players-union-fraud-suit/

18. Fennessy S. The Wright stuff. *Atlanta* magazine [Internet] 2006 Oct. Available from: https://books.google.com/books?id=rQ8AAAAAMBA J&pg=PA142&lpg=PA142&dq=kirk+wright+nfl&source=bl&ots=yZ-len BxlV&sig=ACfU3U1uQBuJzeJ2fTAnfr3sp58qO4bhmw&hl=en&sa=X& ved=2ahUKEwjkttW63bvgAhVOOKwKHZFCATs4ChDoATAIegQIARA B#v=onepage&q=kirk%20wright%20nfl&f=false

19. Ibid.

20. Champion WT. The rise and fall of Kirk Wright: the NFLPA's fiduciary obligation as third-party guarantor of 'certified financial advisors.' [Internet]. Available from: http://mssportslaw.olemiss.edu/files/2015/09/Final-Champion-Edit-1-Macro-p.-1-29.pdf

21. Hrynkiw I. Charles Barkley invested $6.1 million with Donald Watkins, documents in fraud trial show. AL.com [Internet]. 2019 Feb 27. Available from: https://www.al.com/news/birmingham/2019/02/charles-barkleys-adviser-testifies-on-investments-with-watkins.html

22. Whitmire K. An Alabama fraud story: the many faces of Donald Watkins. AL.com [Internet]. 2019 Mar 19. Available from: https://www.al.com/news/2019/03/an-alabama-fraud-story-the-many-faces-of-donald-watkins.html

23. Carlson K, Kim J, Lusardi A, and Camerer CF. Bankruptcy rates among NFL player with short-lived income spikes. *American Economic Review*, American Economic Association. 2015 May;105(5):381–4. 10.3386/w21085

24. Armstrong JS. How to be less persuaded or more persuasive: review of age of propaganda: the everyday use and abuse of persuasion by Anthony Pratkanis and Elliot Aronson. *Journal of Marketing*. 2005 Feb 11;67(1):129–30.

It's the End of the World as We Know It

Men resist randomness, markets resist prophecy.

—Maggie Mahar

On December 17, 1954, *The Chicago Tribune* ran the following headline:

DOCTOR WARNS OF DISASTERS IN WORLD TUESDAY

The paper interviewed Dr. Charles Laughead at the home of Dorothy Martin. Dr. Laughead informed the paper that Martin received communications "from outer space." Reporters were told these communications from outer space revealed to Martin the world would be coming to an end from a great flood. Practically all life on earth would cease to exist in the aftermath, save for the small group of followers who were stationed at Martin's home. Martin convinced her supporters "Supreme Beings" from a planet called Clarion sent her messages promising they would save only the true believers. These messages flowed through her from other planets which would then come out as her own writings which she would relay to her group of fellow flying saucer aficionados.

Dr. Laughead further explained, "There will be a tidal wave, a volcanic action, and a rise in the ground extending from Hudson's Bay [in Canada] to the Gulf of Mexico which will seriously affect the center of the United States. There will be much loss of life, practically all of it, in 1955. It is an actual fact that the world is a mess. But the Supreme Being is going to clean house by sinking all of the land masses as we know them now and raising the land masses now under sea." The doctor further explained that Martin had received intel from the Supreme Being which told her they would be sending a spacecraft to save her group from this cataclysmic event.

The newspaper didn't put much faith in these prophecies as they only ran a short story on page three of the paper that day, but Martin's followers certainly were true believers in her word. She informed her disciples that as long as they followed her teachings they would be spared. This group of roughly 30 people was extremely committed to the cause so they sold all of their possessions, quit their jobs, or stopped going to school in preparation. As the group sat outside of Martin's home on Christmas Eve they sang carols and waited with anticipation for the coming of their saviors. Unfortunately, this was the fourth time the group had been told to wait outside to hitch a ride on the interstellar highway. Each time they waited with bated breath, but their spaceships never arrived.[1]

Each time they didn't show Martin informed her followers of a message that had been relayed from the aliens as a reason for their tardiness. There was always a good excuse, so they convinced themselves each time it didn't happen it must have been a practice session. Martin informed her group the Guardians were to pick them up on the front lawn at midnight on Christmas Eve. When this failed to transpire, the group sat motionless in her living room. They were confused and grasped at straws to come up with reasons for the no-show by their alien brethren. After initially being at a loss for words, Martin finally garnered up the energy to inform the group they had spread so much light that God had saved the world from destruction. *It was a Christmas miracle!*

The members could have chosen to look themselves in the mirror and realize the end-of-the-world prediction was wrong, but that would have required admitting all of the outlandish actions they took and beliefs they held leading up to that point were false. When faced with the prospect of admitting you're wrong or looking for a better explanation, most people get busy looking for an explanation. A few short hours after their failed predictions, Dr. Laughead said the following:

> I've had to go a long way. I've given up just about everything. I've
> cut every tie. I've burned every bridge. I've turned my back on

the world. I can't afford to doubt. I have to believe. And there isn't any other truth.[2]

In *Shawshank Redemption*, Andy Dufresne says, "Get busy living or get busy dying," before making the decision to break out of prison. For people with a strong belief system, that quote looks more like "Get busy living and get busy lying." The day after the spaceship and flood failed to show, the group's members continued to make outlandish prediction after outlandish prediction in hopes at least one of them would come true. There was no soul-searching for what went wrong for the simple reason that these people were far too invested in an outrageous outcome.

One of the members purchased a number of expensive new outfits to wear as many pretty things as she could before the flood came. Another quit her job to live off her life savings. A quote from another member shows just how much conviction they had: "I have to believe the flood is coming on the 21st because I've spent nearly all my money. I quit my job, I quit school, and my apartment costs me $100 a month. I have to believe." They almost all quit their jobs and got rid of their possessions because they truly believed life on Earth was coming to an end and that they would be saved by aliens in a flying saucer.[3]

Cognitive Dissonance

The concept of cognitive dissonance was developed by psychologist Leon Festinger in the 1950s. It arises when a person simultaneously holds two different beliefs that are inconsistent with one another. The theory is that when this happens it causes our minds discomfort, which we then seek to reduce. Whenever this inconsistency in our attitudes, ideas, or opinions kicks in, our default is to eliminate that dissonance. Humans have evolved over time to avoid discomfort, so when we encounter issues that we disagree with it's much easier to simply classify them as being wrong without putting too much thought, effort, or reasoning into it. An alarm bell usually goes off in our head alerting us to this inconsistency, so we give ourselves a mental break to avoid these internal conflicts.

In Festinger's original experiment he asked participants to perform a series of boring tasks for an hour. Once these tasks were finished subjects were supposed to tell another waiting subject that what they were doing was all very exciting to entice them to do the same. They were then separated further into two groups who were paid either $1 or $20 for this acting performance. The researchers found that those who were only paid $1 actually rated their experience performing a dull task as being more enjoyable than the people who were paid $20. The $1 group talked themselves into their actions being enjoyable to reconcile internally with the fact that they wasted time, earned very little, and lied to others about it. This dissonance was only overcome by the false belief that what they did was more enjoyable than it actually was, while the people who were paid $20 were able to recognize they were simply doing it for the money. Basically, cognitive dissonance leads to self-delusion.[4]

Most psychology experiments are conducted in a laboratory or classroom, but Festinger speaks from experience. Festinger and a team of researchers at the University of Minnesota heard about Martin and her followers and decided it would be the perfect opportunity for a real-world study. They earned her confidence in fall of 1954 and were able to infiltrate the house her followers had all gathered in to observe their actions and words leading up to the supposed arrival of the aliens. The researchers not only witnessed this group leading up to their end of the world prediction, but in the aftermath as well. Their research findings were documented in the groundbreaking book *When Prophecy Fails*, which was influential in the study of cognitive dissonance.

A person with conviction is extremely hard to deal with, even when presenting them with alternative facts. Festinger wrote:

> Suppose an individual believes something with his whole heart; suppose further that he has a commitment to this belief, that he has taken irrevocable actions because of it; finally, suppose that he is presented with evidence, unequivocal and undeniable evidence, that his belief is wrong: what will happen? The individual will frequently emerge, not only unshaken, but even more convinced of the truth of his beliefs than ever before. Indeed, he may even show a new fervor about convincing and converting other people to his view.[5]

There was a study performed in the 1980s that exposed a group of people with strongly held positions on social issues to four different arguments on the topic, two pro and two con. For each side of the aisle, there was one argument that was very plausible and another that was wildly implausible. Researchers found people tended to remember the plausible arguments that supported their views and the implausible arguments that went against their views, forsaking the other side.[6]

People latch onto arguments that support what they already believe and ignore even plausible evidence to the contrary. Plus, we tend to seek out implausible arguments only when they strengthen our own opinions. This is why an abundance of information like we have at our disposal today doesn't necessarily change people's minds. There is so much data, analysis, opinions, and information available that you can spin almost any argument in your favor if you so choose. The outcome is almost irrelevant in most cases because your brain is already convinced you're right. Your brain would rather win an argument than get to the bottom of the issue at hand.

You may never find yourself waiting in the cold for a flying saucer to save yourself and your cult friends from an apocalyptic flood, but you will be subject to predictions about the end of the world in other endeavors in life.

The Man Who Walked on Water

At the height of his popularity in the early 1980s, Joe Granville was bringing in over $10 million a year selling investment newsletter subscriptions. The flamboyant market prognosticator traveled around the country giving seminars to drum up business for his service which would send stock market buy and sell recommendations to his subscribers. Granville was well known for his stock market advice, but he was even more well known for his antics at these events.

At a seminar in Tucson, AZ he began walking across the pool on a hidden plank just beneath the water's surface, telling the crowd, "And now you know!" In Atlantic City he was carried in a coffin under a shroud of ticker tape and "resurrected" himself with a martini in hand in front of the crowd.[7] Granville would often drop his pants during speaking gigs to show the audience his boxer shorts which had stock quotes on them. Props such as puppets and clown outfits were often used along with musical instruments. These spectacles kept everyone's attention, but the main event was his predictions about the markets.[8]

Not only did Granville opine on the stock market, he also claimed to follow 33 different earthquake indicators. "If you knew what I knew, you couldn't keep quiet," he claimed while predicting Phoenix would become beachfront property at one point. The forecaster even gave an exact time, 5:31 A.M. PST to be exact, that California should expect an earthquake measuring 8 on the Richter scale to hit. This prediction was based on the alignment of Jupiter, Saturn, and Mercury of course.[9]

But his most famous, or rather infamous, prediction came in early January of 1981. Granville sent a late-night recorded phone message to his 3,000 Early Warning subscribers to "sell everything." The next day was the heaviest trading in the history of the New York Stock Exchange up to that point, with markets falling more than 2%. Granville would appear on the cover of the *New York Times*. The timing of the call couldn't have been worse. Any of his subscribers that followed this prediction missed a face-ripping stock market rally in the early-1980s as Granville stayed bearish while markets almost doubled.[10]

Granville's infamous sell signal in January of 1981 is often panned because of the poor timing but the odd part about this prediction is that the most recent edition of his newsletter, sent to clients just a few days prior, told them to "buy aggressively into the market."[11] After realizing the error of his ways, Granville stated, "I will never make a serious mistake in the stock market again." Narrator: *Yes, he would*. Granville's misses far outweighed his hits for the remainder of the decade. Mark Hulbert has been tracking the performance of investment newsletters for a number of decades. When he looked at Granville's long-term track record of performance from market-timing calls, he found from 1980 through January 2005, Granville's stock tips lost almost 1% a year compared to a 12% annual gain for the stock market in that time. His more aggressive recommendations lost 10% *per year* in that time.[12]

Granville has had plenty of company over the years in terms of people who were so sure of their prediction systems yet were flat out wrong. Near the bottom of the brutal bear market in 1974, James Dines, another investment newsletter publisher, took out an ad proclaiming "THE DINES LETTER HAS NEVER BEEN SO BEARISH." Dines claimed, "We're gonna have a full-scale collapse within the next six months. There may be violence in the streets." Over the next year the Dow went much higher, from 600 to 1,000. There was no full-scale collapse.

In 1982, magazine ads from William Finnegan, a computer trading firm in California, made the following promise:

> If you happen to know what the Dow Jones Average will be 80 trading days from now, you could make quite an impression on your friends. Not to mention your banker. Well, you can know.

To gain this knowledge about the future price of the Dow, you had to buy a computer program that would then spit out the market outlook for the next 80 days. When the model was initially rolled out, every single day for the next 80 days, Finnegan's model predicted a market decline. The first day was a prediction of a 7.5% loss. Instead the market was up 1,000 points during those 80 days.[13]

No One Knows What's Going to Happen

In Granville's defense, he was more of an entertainer than an actual investment advisor. He even admitted to the *Wall Street Journal* in 1989, "I observed that when people are entertained, they will retain more information." Another time Granville observed people retain three times as much information when they're entertained.[14] There's a huge difference between prediction and advice, but most people latch onto predictions because they're sexier. Forecasts may be exciting but they tell you nothing about what the future has in store.

Linton Wells was an expert in national security and served in a number of different roles in the White House under both Bill Clinton and George W. Bush. As the Deputy Assistant Secretary of Defense to President Bush, Wells published a memo titled "Thoughts for the 2001 Quadrennial Defense Review." It looked at the state of the world at the beginning of each decade starting with the year 1900. The memo read:

- If you had been a security policy-maker in the world's greatest power in 1900, you would have been a Brit, looking warily at your age-old enemy, France.
- By 1910, you would be allied with France and your enemy would be Germany.
- By 1920, World War I would have been fought and won, and you'd be engaged in a naval arms race with your erstwhile allies, the US and Japan.
- By 1930, naval arms limitation treaties were in effect, the Great Depression was underway, and the defense planning standard said, "no war for ten years."
- Nine years later, World War II had begun.
- By 1950, Britain no longer the world's greatest power, the Atomic Age had dawned, and a "police action" was underway in Korea.
- Ten years later the political focus was on the "missile gap," the strategic paradigm was shifting from massive retaliation to flexible response, and few people had heard of Vietnam.

- By 1970, the peak of our involvement in Vietnam had come and gone, we were beginning detente with the Soviets, and we were anointing the Shah as our protege in the Gulf Region.
- By 1980, the Soviets were in Afghanistan, Iran was in the throes of revolution, there was talk of our "hollow forces" and a "window of vulnerability," and the US was the greatest creditor nation the world had ever seen.
- By 1990, the Soviet Union was within a year of dissolution, American forces in the desert were on the verge of showing they were anything but hollow, the US had become the greatest debtor nation the world had ever known, and almost no one had heard of the Internet.
- Ten years later, Warsaw was the capital of a NATO nation, asymmetric threats transcended geography, and the parallel revolutions of information, biotechnology, robotics, nanotechnology, and high-density energy sources foreshadowed changes almost beyond forecasting.
- All of which is to say that I'm not sure what 2010 will look like, but I'm sure that it will be very little like we expect, so we should plan accordingly.

This was sent to the President a mere six months before 9/11 turned the world upside down. The decade that followed included war, political turmoil, the Great Financial Crisis, and countless geopolitical crises around the globe. The one constant we face as a species is irreducible uncertainty. It doesn't matter if you're Jeff Bezos, George Soros, or the President of the United States. No one has a clue what the future holds.

Of course, that doesn't stop us from trying to guess what's going to happen in the future. In many ways, our actions on a daily basis are based on forecasts whether we admit it or not. We forecast our relationships, our careers, our finances, and our interactions with other people. But there is a huge difference between being right about how the future will play out, and success in the markets or business world.

Philip Tetlock is an expert in tracking the forecasts of, well, other experts. Going back to the 1980s, Tetlock tracked the results of tournaments of 300 or so forecasters, who were experts in a wide variety of fields. This group made around 30,000 predictions about geopolitics, economics, and markets over a two-decade period. Tetlock discovered these experts were wrong more often than they were right. Not only that, but they would have been more accurate had they simply assigned an equal probability to the outcomes they were trying to predict. Predictions made further out into the future were less accurate than short-term forecasts. The same was true for extreme predictions. Maybe the most surprising finding of all is the greater the level of expertise, the lower the accuracy of the forecaster. There was even an inverse relationship between how well forecasters thought they were doing and how well they actually did. Knowing a lot about a subject can actually make a person a worse forecaster than simply knowing a little. Experts do play a vital role in society in a number of ways, but predicting the future is not one of them.[15]

Why Pessimism Sells Better than Optimism

Columnist Franklin Pierce Adams once observed, "Nothing is more responsible for the good old days than a bad memory." Joe Granville may have had a bearish bent to his predictions because his father had bad memories of the worst crash of all time. His father was a banker who lost it all in the market crash during the Great Depression. Granville once said, "It wasn't the market that did it. It was Wall Street. If he had followed what I teach, he'd have made $8 million on the Crash."[16]

End-of-the-world predictions, whether we're talking about the actual world, the markets, or the economy, will always find an audience because negativity sells better than positivity to most people. Negative stories stick with us longer than positive stories. Look no further than the news every single day to understand this phenomenon. Good news and bad news play out over completely different time horizons because bad news happens fast while good news is gradual.

As Bill Gates once said: "Headlines, in a way, are what mislead you, because bad news is a headline, and gradual improvement is not." You can't blame the news industry because it would sound odd if they reported more good news than bad news. The economist Max Roser once pointed out that the following headline could have been read every day for the past 25 years:

NUMBER OF PEOPLE IN EXTREME POVERTY FELL BY 137,000 SINCE YESTERDAY

This is an unbelievable achievement that no one cares about on a daily basis because it's a process, not an event. The fact that we now live in a 24-hour news cycle has made it even harder for optimism to find its way into the news. Good news is incongruous with attention.

Steven Pinker, a psychology professor at Harvard, has written extensively about the fact that (1) the world is getting better over time but (2) most people assume the world is getting worse. Pinker tells us why the market is so vast for pessimistic experts:

> Irrational pessimism is also driven by a morbid interest in what can go wrong – and there are always more ways for things to go wrong than to go right. This creates a market for experts to remind us of things that can go wrong that we may have overlooked. Biblical prophets, op-ed pundits, social critics, dystopian filmmakers and tabloid psychics know they can achieve instant gravitas by warning of an imminent doomsday. Those who point out that the world is getting better – even hardheaded analysts who are just reading out the data – may be dismissed as starry-eyed naïfs.[17]

We look at an optimist as someone who's stating the obvious while a pessimist is someone who isn't wrong, just early. Pessimism feels more intelligent while optimism makes you feel like part of the intelligent crowd.

The Value of 'I Don't Know'

On the late-night show *Jimmy Kimmel Live*, they used to do a bit called Lie Witness News where Kimmel would go out to Hollywood Boulevard and interview people on the street about current events. In 2014, he set out to find self-proclaimed soccer fans during the World Cup. Kimmel asked a number of people how US star Landon Donovan was performing during that year's World Cup in Brazil. Here are some of the responses, again from people who claim to be huge soccer fans:

> "He's good. He's still got one more in him."
> "I've seen him play way better in the World Cup so I know he's underachieving right now."

The problem with their analysis is that Landon Donovan was cut from the US team before the World Cup even began. Donovan didn't play a single match in the 2014 World Cup because he wasn't on the team. To be fair, Kimmel's production team likely set these people up by choosing the most confident of the bunch. I'm sure there are plenty of people who would say or do almost anything to get on TV.

But research by behavioral psychologists and everyday experiences with almost any human being on the planet point to the fact that we all have the ability to be overconfident idiots at times. This is called the Dunning-Kruger Effect, which is the idea that we all have difficulty in recognizing our own incompetence in certain areas. Warren Buffett has laid out two simple rules for investing, "Rule Number 1: Never lose money. Rule Number 2: Never forget rule number one." For the Dunning-Kreuger Effect the two simple rules go something like this:

Rule Number 1: Everyone is an overconfident idiot from time to time.
Rule Number 2: Always forget rule number 1 when I'm the one being an idiot.

To overcome the fact that we can all act like overconfident idiots, Charles Darwin created a golden rule whenever he came across ideas that were inconsistent with his theories. Darwin would immediately write down those observations that were in conflict with his work to be able to see the other side in case he was wrong. In his autobiography, Darwin wrote, "For I had found by experience that such facts and thoughts were far more apt to escape from memory than the favourable ones." Many groups of people these days are more concerned with winning than being right. It's not easy because your brain will naturally fight news and opinions you don't agree with, but having an open mind doesn't cost you anything.

Avoid people who look at the world through the lens of certainty, especially about the future. It's always best to think about future events through a probabilistic lens. Forecasting expert Tetlock concluded in his study of experts by stating, "There is often a curiously inverse relationship between how well forecasters thought they were doing and how well they did."[18]

Predicting the future is an unattainable goal, but humility and self-awareness are both within everyone's grasp.

Notes

1. Doctor warns of disasters in world Tuesday. *Chicago Tribune.* 1954 Dec 17.
2. Festinger L, Riecken HW, and Schachter S. *When Prophecy Fails: A Social and Psychological Study of a Modern Group That Predicted the Destruction of the World.* New York: Harper-Torchbooks; 1956.

3. Ibid.
4. Festinger L. *A Theory of Cognitive Dissonance*. Stanford: Stanford University Press; 1957.
5. Ibid.
6. Wright R. *The Moral Animal: Why We Are, the Way We Are*. New York: Pantheon; 1994.
7. Brimelow P. *The Wall Street Gurus: How You Can Profit from Investment Newsletters*. New York: Random House; 1986.
8. Drew C. Joseph E. Granville, stock market predictor, dies at 90. *The New York Times* [Internet] 2013 Sep 18. Available from: https://www.nytimes.com/2013/09/19/business/joseph-e-granville-stock-market-predictor-dies-at-90.html
9. McMurran K. When Joe Granville speaks, small wonder that the market yo-yos and tickers fibrillate. *People* [Internet]. 1981 Apr 6. Available from: https://people.com/archive/when-joe-granville-speaks-small-wonder-that-the-market-yo-yos-and-tickers-fibrillate-vol-15-no-13/
10. Brimelow P. *The Wall Street Gurus: How You Can Profit from Investment Newsletters*. New York: Random House; 1986.
11. Hammer AR. Stocks decline sharply as trading soars to record. *The New York Times* [Internet]. 1981 Jan 8. Available from: https://www.nytimes.com/1981/01/08/business/stocks-decline-sharply-as-trading-soars-to-record.html
12. Brimelow P. *The Wall Street Gurus: How You Can Profit from Investment Newsletters*. New York: Random House; 1986.
13. Train J. *Famous Financial Fiascos*. New York: Random House; 1984.
14. Miller S. Granville was market timer with flair. *The Wall Street Journal* [Internet]. 2013 Sep 10. Available from: https://www.wsj.com/articles/granville-was-market-timer-with-flair-1378854096
15. Tetlock P. *Expert Political Judgment: How Good is It? How Can We Know?* New Jersey: Princeton University Press; 2017.
16. McMurran K. When Joe Granville speaks, small wonder that the market yo-yos and tickers fibrillate. *People* [Internet]. 1981 Apr 6. Available from: https://people.com/archive/when-joe-granville-speaks-small-wonder-that-the-market-yo-yos-and-tickers-fibrillate-vol-15-no-13/
17. Pinker S. Harvard professor Steven Pinker on why we refuse to see the bright side, even though we should. *Time* [Internet] 2018 Jan 4. Available from: http://time.com/5087384/harvard-professor-steven-pinker-on-why-we-refuse-to-see-the-bright-side/
18. Tetlock P. *Expert Political Judgment: How Good is It? How can we know?* New Jersey: Princeton University Press; 2017.

CHAPTER 5

Sleight of Hand

The greatest trick the devil ever pulled was convincing the world he didn't exist.

—Verbal Kint

By her mid-20s, Molly Bloom transitioned from one of the highest ranked members of the US ski team to running the show in Hollywood's biggest underground poker game, where tables included the likes of Spiderman, Batman, and Jack Dawson. How she ever got to that point is a story made for Hollywood. Bloom grew up in a ski family in Colorado. Her brother, Jeremy, was a three-time World Champion and two-time Olympic freestyle skier who also played football for the University of Colorado and Philadelphia Eagles. Molly Bloom was a member of the US Ski Team and ranked as high as third in all North America by the late 1990s.

When she shut down her skiing career, Bloom decided to head to California to see if she could cut it in Tinseltown. After bouncing around from job to job she ended up working as the assistant to a real estate developer. This developer had some connections to the entertainment industry which led to a weekly poker game with some high rollers. One of Bloom's new roles was to run those games for him and his friends. Those friends just happened to be some of the most well-known actors in the world, along with a number of others from the entertainment industry, professional sports, and the business world. Regulars at these poker games included Leonardo DiCaprio, Tobey Maguire, Ben Affleck, director Todd Phillips, real estate magnate Bob Safai, Houston Rockets owner Leslie Alexander, Alex Rodriguez, and one of the owners of the Los Angeles Dodgers.[1]

There are a number of reasons so many high rollers were attracted to these secretive poker games. The fact that they were played outside of a regulated setting meant they could play for high stakes. Buy-ins were as large as $100,000, and it wasn't uncommon for annual profits and losses to hit seven figures for certain players. Tobey Maguire, who played the original Spiderman, apparently gloated after one of Bloom's games, "I'm going to make $10 million this year on poker."[2]

Bloom was paid handsomely to set up posh hotel suites for the games, hire the dealers, ensure bodyguards were in place, keep track of profits and losses for each player, and arrange for payments to be made after the games. The games were held at some of the most luxurious hotels in Beverly Hills. The exclusivity and privacy of the game allowed players to speak freely about money, investments, art, wine, and everything in between at the tables. Bloom ensured the players had anything they wanted and more including massages, private chefs, and bottle service on hand. The nice digs and private setting helped make the players comfortable, but the biggest reason hundreds of thousands of dollars could be won or lost on a single hand had more to do with ego, competition, confidence, and power. Bloom wrote in her tell-all book:

> There's something that happens to people when they see the opportunity to make money. Greed flavored with desperation, especially at a poker table, gives rise to a moment when the eyes change, the humanity vanishes, and the players become bloodthirsty, flat-eyed predators.[3]

The only reason Bloom was able to run such a game outside of a casino setting is the way she structured her business. She didn't make money the way the house does at a casino by taking a vig or percentage of the wagers. Instead, Bloom earned money strictly from tips paid by the wealthy players in her game. And those tips weren't of the garden variety. It's estimated Bloom was raking in almost $30,000 a night for her services. She even sought counsel from a lawyer, who told her she was operating in a gray area, and that Bloom should not break the law while she was kind of sort of breaking the law. For an underground gambling ring, things were surprisingly above board.

The fact she was making so much irked some of the players, especially Maguire, so her LA game eventually flamed out.[4] Not wanting to let the momentum slip, Bloom took her talents to the Big Apple to set up a similar game in New York City for the east coast high rollers. The NYC poker scene wasn't as big as the LA games so it was during this transition that Bloom began taking rakes from the games, a big no-no in the eyes of law enforcement. The gray area she was operating in before was no more – this was now an illegal gambling operation. At one point the Russian mob asked to get in on the action. When she politely declined their offer, a mobster showed up at her door, stuck a gun in her mouth, beat and robbed her, and claimed payback for turning down his pals.

Surprisingly, none of these actions were what caused the FBI to bring charges against Bloom for her role in orchestrating these high stakes poker games. It was something else no one saw coming.

Bad Brad

In 2006, a hedge fund manager named Bradley Ruderman wanted to join Bloom's LA game to hobnob with the Hollywood elite. Ruderman seemed harmless enough, with an affable attitude and plenty of money to throw around. The biggest reason the players let him into their underground scene was the fact he was terrible at poker and had a lot of money. In fact, his nickname at the table was "Bad Brad." Although the high rollers enjoyed a competitive game, no one minded taking money on a regular basis from a rich hedge fund manager who didn't seem to care he seemingly lost every time he sat down at the table. It would take years for the regulars to realize Ruderman was playing a game within a game.

In her autobiography Bloom said Ruderman was the worst poker player she had ever seen.

"He lost buy-in after buy-in, until almost everyone at the table was up and he was the financier. The players were looking at me in disbelief as the feeding frenzy ran its course," she said.

Bloom claimed it was a running joke for the rest of the players to text her "Is Brad playing?"[5] before each game. Bad Brad was so terrible at poker everyone considered it free money when he sat down. It was like he was trying to lose. While Ruderman later claimed he became addicted to gambling, he had ulterior motives for continuing to show up and lose his money – he needed new investors for his hedge fund. The poker game was the perfect place to find wealthy individuals to invest in his hedge fund. There was so much one-upmanship and envy involved it ended up being fertile breeding ground for wealthy marks.

Ruderman played the perfect patsy by "donating" his money to the other players. The poker losses were chump change in comparison to the money he could make from the fees charged to new investors in his hedge fund. And as it turns out, it wasn't just exorbitant hedge fund fees he was looking for. Ruderman was running a $44 million Ponzi scheme by scamming friends, family members, and rich Hollywood types out of their money. The new investors in the fund were necessary to keep up the charade to pay off the old investors.

Talk at the tables invariably turned to business and the financial matters. Ruderman claimed his hedge fund was returning up to 60% a year. In fact, according to the lawsuit filed by the SEC, these were the annual returns Ruderman showed to his clients and prospects:

Year	Percentage Gain
2002	55.99%
2003	60.56%
2004	32.17%
2005	23.30%
2006	22.02%
2007	19.09%
2008	14.99%

Figure 5.1   Bad Brad's Reported Hedge Fund Returns

These gains are so otherworldly that warning bells should have been going off in people's heads immediately. When things are going well investors tend to loosen up their due diligence in hopes that what seems too-good-to-be-true may in fact be true just for them. The history of financial scams is littered with examples of everything working until a market crash hits. Much like Bernie Madoff, Brad Ruderman was exposed by the 2008 stock market crash and deep recession. Bull markets can sustain even the worst of financial frauds. Bear markets make it difficult for even the best of scams to hold up. Not only was his Ponzi scheme unravelling, but Ruderman was in so deep that his losses at the poker table eventually turned into real money.

Court filings show Bad Brad lost close to $5.2 million in high-stake poker games while trying to bring more clients into his fund. Like most gamblers and investors who find themselves staring at huge losses, Ruderman actually thought he could play his way out of his slump to at least break even. He kept up the charade until March 2009, which was the month before his fund was forced to declare bankruptcy. It's fitting that the stock market bottomed from the enormous crash that very same month. Among the biggest losers in Ruderman's Ponzi scheme was Tom Gores, the billionaire owner of the Detroit Pistons.[6]

Once his scam came to light and he was convicted in 2009, the high rollers in the secret poker game were outed in the press. In a court deposition, Ruderman named Maguire, Alex Rodriguez, and director Nick Cassavetes as the players he lost the most money to in Bloom's game.[7] During that deposition, Ruderman admitted, "I'm thinking like any gambler is thinking or any pathological gambler is thinking. You're not keeping track of the actual numbers. You're thinking, I'm that much closer to going on the big run. That's the juice." This guy was one of the worst poker players and hedge fund managers in the world, but he still thought his luck was sure to change if he just kept at it. Not only was he losing money, but he was taking client money directly out of his funds and using that cash for personal use.[8]

Bloom was subpoenaed because Ruderman claimed he became addicted to gambling through her games, which led him to lose sight of his morals. That slippery slope led to the Ponzi scheme.[9] Legal documents show Ruderman himself paid Bloom nearly $500,000 in tips for her poker services in a little over a year-and-a-half of play.[10] Bloom made for a convenient scapegoat but it doesn't sound like Bad

Brad needed much help pushing his morals to the limits. The FBI determined Ruderman spent almost $9 million of client funds over the course of his fraud. This included a beach house in Malibu, two Porsches, and a handful of tickets to professional sporting events.[11]

Ruderman told investors in the fund he had more than $800 million of capital invested. In reality, there was only $650,000 in assets. Bad Brad roped in a few clients by claiming Lowell Milken, chairman of the Milken Foundation and brother of financier Michael Milken, and Oracle CEO Larry Ellison were investors in the fund. This was a lie. Neither had money invested in the fund. It was a ruse to get wealthy people to invest based on the idea that other wealthy people were invested. Unbelievably, for a number of his clients from name recognition alone.

By early 2009, things got so bad that Ruderman was forced to use new investor funds to pay early investors off who needed their money back because of the financial crisis.[12] The only reason Bloom was roped into the legal proceedings is because the duped investors in Ruderman's ill-fated hedge fund believed they could claw back some of their money that was lost at the poker table. She pled guilty to some minor charges and was sentenced to a year of probation, some community service, and a small fine. Bad Brad would spend eight years in jail.[13]

A Magician Reveals His Secrets

In any financial chicanery there is almost always a game within a game being played. Every fraud includes some combination of a good story, loose morals, and some misdirection. In the early 1900s, brothers Fred and Charley Gondorff would set up a swanky gambling den in a posh hotel suite in New York City, much like Molly Bloom would do more than a century later. The Gondorff brothers wore tuxedos to look like wealthy men, which attracted other rich people to their games. It's amazing how time and time again in these stories, it is so easy to lure in wealthy victims simply by playing up their insecurities about wealth. It's almost as if flaunting wealth is like a fishing lure for other wealthy people. The brothers' marks were always happy to play a few hands to better their social standing. They would invariably end up losing in a rigged game of poker that the brothers had set up. These rigged games made the brothers more than $15 million over a 15-year period using a variation of this scam.[14]

Ruderman's sleight of hand involved losing money to rich people to make himself look so wealthy that it didn't matter how much he lost at the table. Maybe it should have been a red flag that a hedge fund manager who promised such high returns in the markets could be such an awful poker player, but he was obviously able to bluff his way into enough accredited investor (read: rich people) capital that he knew how to make a decent investment pitch. People should know better than to trust outlandish returns in the financial markets, but our brains work against us when trying to set realistic expectations. We're not well suited to see sleight of hand even when it's right in front of us.

Norman Triplett used slight of hand to fool people for a living. Triplett published a paper called, "The Psychology of Conjuring Deceptions," in 1900 in which he revealed the secrets behind some of the greatest magic tricks of that day. One of his experiments was used to show how easily our brains can be tricked through sleight of hand. A magician went to several classrooms and sat behind a desk while throwing a ball up in the air three times in succession. The first throw was about three feet in the air. When the ball dropped the magician would let his hands fall just below the desk so they were hidden from the audience. The next throw was four to five feet in the air but at this point when it came down it was placed between the magician's legs and concealed. So on the final attempt the magician made a throwing motion but the ball never actually left his lap. As he made the movement with his arm he pretended to watch it go into the air and then, poof, the ball disappeared, at least for many members of the audience.

This wasn't exactly a David Blaine-esque magic trick but it was surprisingly effective on a number of people who witnessed it. The researchers had the participants in the classroom write down what they saw and when they realized the ball had vanished. There were 165 people in all who watched the vanishing ball trick. Seventy-eight of them claimed they saw the ball go up and flat-out disappear from sight. Here are some of their responses:

> I saw it come two times. It was about halfway up to the ceiling before it disappeared.
> I saw it come down, but not the last. It was about one foot.
> I did not see the ball come down. It was halfway to the ceiling before it disappeared.

Triplett studied this illusion on a number of different occasions and came to the conclusion that confidence by the magician is the chief quality that inspires people to be fooled. But he also tried to get more scientific by stating, "What the audience sees is an image of repetition, which is undoubtedly partly the effect of a residual stimulation in the eye, partly a central excitation."[15]

His repetition theory does seem grounded in reality considering research shows our brains automatically and unconsciously expect to see a third repetition after we see two in a row of something.[16] However, the technology wasn't available at the time to test Triplett's assumptions, which is why Gustav Kuhn, a modern-day magician, decided to test Triplett's theory using more current methods. Kuhn tested out two versions of the vanishing ball trick to pin down why so many people assumed the ball had vanished right before their eyes.

For the first experiment, he performed the trick exactly as Triplett had done it, throwing the ball up in the air twice before secretly hanging on to the ball and pretending to throw it on the last attempt. Kuhn also made sure to have his own eyes follow the path of the imaginary ball. This allowed him to test out another version of the trick, wherein everything else was carried out in the same way as the original version but this time he didn't watch it go up, instead looking down at his other hand.

Using some fancy equipment which wasn't available in the early 1900s, Kuhn was able to measure the eye movements of the participants in his study. In the first version, roughly two-thirds of participants experienced the illusion of the ball disappearing and claimed to have seen the magician throwing it on the third attempt. They assumed someone else must have caught the ball or that it had to be a trick ball that somehow stuck to the ceiling. When they watched the video these people were astounded to see what actually happened. In their minds, that third throw was real.

The power of a simple gaze was important in selling the illusion. The second version of the trick was far less effective when he didn't watch the imaginary ball go up in the air. It's the "fake throw the ball" game that everyone has played with their dog at one time or another. If you don't sell it, the trick isn't nearly as effective. Kuhn's findings illustrate this simple illusion was driven by expectations. When he and his researchers looked more closely at the video of the audience during the trick, most people were looking at the face of the magician, even though they claimed to be watching the ball. They were taking a short cut by looking at his face instead of watching the actual ball.

In his book, *Experiencing the Impossible,* Kuhn concluded, "Our brain uses a really clever and almost science-fictional trick that prevents us from living in the past: we look into the future. Our visual system is continuously predicting the future, and the world that you are now perceiving is the world that your visual system has predicted to be the present in the past."[17]

In other words, unless you're someone who is actually able to predict the future (trust me, you're not), then you will always be experiencing the past in many ways during the present because our memories shape so much of what we see. This is why investors are so enamored with enormous reported performance numbers from hedge fund managers like Brad Ruderman. Most investments come with the standard disclaimer that "past performance is not indicative of future results." But many investors love to believe the opposite is true. And that's exactly why investment frauds using made-up return streams will never go away.

We want to believe those numbers are true, and not just in the past for other investors, but for ourselves well into the future. Magical return numbers will always draw people in, but it's best to be skeptical when anyone makes outlandish promises for outsized returns.

Notes

1. Masters K and Miller D. The secret world of Hollywood poker. *The Hollywood Reporter* [Internet]. 2011 Sep 21. Available from: https://www.hollywoodreporter.com/news/hollywood-poker-tobey-maguire-alex-rodriguez-241603
2. Storey K. Inside the underground world of celebrity poker. *New York Post* [Internet]. 2014 Jun 22. Available from: https://nypost.com/2014/06/22/inside-the-poker-princess-a-list-house-of-cards/
3. Bloom, M. Molly's game: the true story of the 26-year-old woman behind the most exclusive, high stakes underground poker game in the world. New York: HaperCollins; 2014.
4. Kolker R. Manhattan fold 'em. New York [Internet]. 2013 Jul 8. Available from: http://nymag.com/news/features/gambling-ring-2013-7/index3.html
5. Bloom, M. *Molly's Game: The True Story of the 26-Year-Old Woman Behind the Most Exclusive, High Stakes Underground Poker Game in the World.* New York: HarperCollins; 2014.
6. Masters K and Miller D. The secret world of Hollywood poker. *The Hollywood Reporter* [Internet]. 2011 Sep 21. Available from: https://www.hollywoodreporter.com/news/hollywood-poker-tobey-maguire-alex-rodriguez-241603

7. Kolker R. Manhattan fold 'em. *New York* magazine [Internet]. 2013 Jul 8. Available from: http://nymag.com/news/features/gambling-ring-2013-7/index3.html

8. Howard D. Ponzi mastermind who lost clients' millions in Hollywood poker breaks silence: new details inside games played by Tobey Maguire, Ben Affleck and Matt Damon. Celebuzz! [Internet]. 2012 Aug 13. Available from: https://www.celebuzz.com/2012-08-13/ponzi-mastermind-who-lost-clients-millions-in-hollywood-poker-breaks-silence-new-details-inside-games-played-by-tobey-maguire-ben-affleck-and-matt-damon/

9. Bloom, M. *Molly's Game: The True Story of the 26-Year-Old Woman Behind the Most Exclusive, High Stakes Underground Poker Game in the World.* New York: HarperCollins; 2014.

10. Masters K and Miller D. The secret world of Hollywood poker. *The Hollywood Reporter* [Internet]. 2011 Sep 21. Available from: https://www.hollywoodreporter.com/news/hollywood-poker-tobey-maguire-alex-rodriguez-241603

11. Hedge fund manager who bilked relatives out of $25 million sentenced to over 10 years in federal prison. The Federal Bureau of Investigation [Internet]. 2010 Jan 11. Available from: https://archives.fbi.gov/archives/losangeles/press-releases/2010/la011110a.htm

12. SEC halts Beverly Hills hedge fund fraud. Securities and Exchange Commission v. Bradley L. Ruderman, Ruderman Capital Management, LLC, Ruderman Capital Partners, LLC, and Ruderman Capital Partners A, LLC, Civil Action No. CV 09-02974 VBF (JCx) (C.D. Cal.) Litigation Release No. 21017. 2009 Apr 29. Available from: https://www.sec.gov/litigation/litreleases/2009/lr21017.htm

13. Howard D. Ponzi mastermind who lost clients' millions in Hollywood poker breaks silence: new details inside games played by Tobey Maguire, Ben Affleck and Matt Damon. Celebuzz! [Internet]. 2012 Aug 13. Available from: https://www.celebuzz.com/2012-08-13/ponzi-mastermind-who-lost-clients-millions-in-hollywood-poker-breaks-silence-new-details-inside-games-played-by-tobey-maguire-ben-affleck-and-matt-damon/

14. Nash JR. *Hustlers and Con Men: An Anecdotal History of the Confidence Man and His games.* New York: M. Evans & Company; 1976.

15. Triplett N. The psychology of conjuring deceptions. *The American Journal of Psychology.* 1900 Jul;10(4):439–510. doi: 10.2307/1412365

16. Zweig, J. *Your Money and Your Brain: How the New Science of Neuroeconomics Can Make You Rich.* New York: Simon & Schuster; 2007.

17. Kuhn, G. *Experiencing the Impossible: The Science of Magic.* Cambridge, MA: MIT Press; 2019.

CHAPTER 6

When Success Doesn't Translate

Experience is the worst teacher. It gives the test before giving the lesson.

—Jim Paul

Back in my college days, my friends and I would go on an annual canoe trip down the Manistee River every spring in the middle of nowhere in Northern Michigan. It was something of a last hurrah before school was out for the summer. During my final trip down the river before graduating we were picked up and driven back to our campsite by the owners of the canoe rental shop after a long day in the sun. A group of us began to wax philosophical with the canoe rental owner, a guy in his mid-to-late 30s.

He shared with us what it was like living in a rural area with his wife and young child. It was a simple, minimalist lifestyle. They lived in a small, beat-up trailer, didn't have many material possessions, and didn't make a lot of money from the canoe rental business. They both had to pick up odd jobs in the winter to stay afloat.

This was during the tail end of my college experience when my peers and I were looking for our first jobs. We were all worried about how much money we were going to make and the status of the jobs we would land. I remember being struck by this guy and his wife, living a very simple life in the middle of nowhere, but being completely satisfied with what they had. They got to work outside during the summer and be on the water all day. Their work schedules were flexible, and they were their own bosses. They worked together and got to spend quality time with each other every day. They didn't have much in the way of material possessions, but they didn't want for much either. Their story has always stuck with me because it showed success and happiness in life don't always follow the same exact path for everyone.

Having a rich life means different things to different people. There are a multitude of ways to find happiness at different income levels or standards of living. But one sure way to ensure you'll never be totally satisfied with your life or your financial situation is if you're constantly caught up in the allure of more. Financial writer Nick Murray once wrote, "No matter how much money you have, if you're still worried, you aren't wealthy."[1]

Having a high net worth and living a rich life are two completely different things. A survey of people with a net worth of at least $25 million (excluding their primary residence) found almost one-quarter of this group said they worry "constantly" about their financial situation.[2] Happiness researcher Michael Norton interviewed more than 2,000 people who have a net worth of $1 million or more to ask them how happy they were on a scale of 1 to 10. He then asked how much more money it would take to get them to go from their current level to a 10. Norton said, "All the way up the income-wealth spectrum basically everyone says [they'd need] two or three times as much" to be perfectly happy. [3]

In some ways this says a lot about the human desire for progress and the will to improve your place in life. But there's also something to be said for contentment and the ability to appreciate what you have, especially when you've already achieved some level of success in your life, financial or otherwise. The problem is there will always be someone wealthier or more successful than you, so the comparisons will never stop if you allow them to take over how you view your standing in life. This allure of more can become a never-ending phenomenon, even for the most successful among us.

Defeated by Decency

Ulysses S. Grant is one of the great war strategists in history. Military historian John Keegan said of Grant, he "was the greatest general of war, one who would have excelled at any time in any army."[4] His time just so happened to coincide with a major turning point in American history, the Civil War. Grant was the architect of the North's victory. After Lincoln's assassination, he held the country together and made sure the 15th amendment was upheld so African Americans would have the right to vote. Grant finished Lincoln's mission to keep slavery illegal. Famous wordsmith Walt Whitman once wrote, "Out of all the hubbub of the war, Lincoln and Grant emerge, the towering majestic figures."[5]

Grant's honor served him well on the battlefield, but it likely worked against him as a politician and businessman once his military days were over, leading the great general to be far too trusting of speculators and charlatans. While in office as president, Grant succumbed to Jay Gould's scheming ways. Gould was a ruthless businessman and speculator who tried to take advantage of Grant to earn a profit. "The people had *desired* money," before Gould, Mark Twain observed, "but *he* taught them to fall down and worship it."[6] Gould drummed up a scheme to corner the market in gold in 1869 by driving up its price through actions by the Treasury. Gould had been secretly stockpiling the yellow metal for months before convincing Grant it made fiscal sense for the US to avoid selling its gold reserves. With the Treasury out of the way as the biggest seller in the market, speculators could drive up the price, which is exactly what they did. Grant finally caught on and when the Treasury flooded the market by selling, prices crashed. The stock market also fell 20%, ruining many a financial institution and even impacting the economy.[7]

Grant was not a wealthy man going into the White House, nor was he a wealthy man coming out of the White House, but he was certainly better off than most. After serving two terms as president from 1869–1877, he was unable to fund his own retirement, mostly because he sacrificed his military pension to run for office. A group of bankers on Wall Street set up a $250,000 fund to give him enough money for a retirement fitting a former president and one of the most decorated war generals in history. Donors even gave him $100,000 to buy a house on Fifth Avenue in NYC. This probably should have been enough, but Grant wanted more.

Eager to find his place in the business world, Grant entered into a partnership with 29-year-old Ferdinand Ward. Their financial company would be called Grant and Ward. Ward was called the "Young Napoleon of Finance." Grant assumed it wouldn't be long until he

was a millionaire based strictly on Ward's mind for business and finance. To get the venture off the ground, Grant put up $50,000.
Ward and another banker were supposed to put up their own seed
capital as well, but it turned out Grant was the only founder who
actually ponied up any cash. The partnership was off to an ominous
start, but little did Grant know it was about to get a whole lot worse.[8]

The biggest problem with the business plan for Grant and Ward
was that there was no business plan. Ward promised to deliver early
investors 15–20% returns a *month* in profits. To put this into perspective, that's an annualized return of 400–800% a year! Yet few of
the investors bothered to question how they could earn such juicy
returns. And when investors did ask how he made such enormous
profits, Ward would tell them he had large government contracts for
commodities which Grant worked out in secret. These contracts, of
course, did not exist in the slightest.

Grant was more or less a figurehead for the company. He didn't
have any real-world business experience, so his sole job was to bring
in more investors. Union veterans poured money into the fund
based on Grant's name alone. Ward had unlimited power in running the firm, signing the checks and running the books himself, a
common theme that runs through many financial scams. Grant never reviewed any of the transactions or hired a lawyer to look at the
business agreement. He often signed letters written by Ward without
bothering to read them first. The former president never looked at
the books, just the monthly statements produced by Ward, which he
assumed were satisfactory. Grant boasted about the returns to others
but never had an inkling as to how they were made. He told his wife
not to worry about setting aside money for their children's future.
"Ward is making us all rich – them as well as ourselves." When asked
how business was going, Grant replied, "I think we have made more
money during the past year than any other house in Wall Street." He
sang Ward's praises calling him the "ablest young businessman he
ever saw." Ward was showered with gifts from the famous general including leopard skins, Japanese swords, and hand-painted bamboo
screens, all from Grant's tours around the globe. Grant even kept a
pair of his family's horses at Ward's stables.[9]

Little did he know, behind his back Ward called Grant a "child in
business matters" and figured he would never be able to uncover the
fraud Ward was quietly performing. Ward was described as having a
"psychopath's ability to counterfeit sincerity and present the exact

image other people wanted to see." After he was warned by a friend about suspect profits in the business, Grant replied, "These are able and experienced businessmen who are engaged with Ward. They would not be likely to take part in any foolish scheme."[10]

Yogi Berra once said, "I don't want to belong to any club that would accept me as a member." That should have been Grant's rule of thumb when looking at the world of business deals. Ward began piling up enormous debts by using the same securities as collateral for multiple loans and he alone had access to those securities. While Grant was living it up spending money like it was going out of business, Ward was literally making sure they would go out of business. Ward was constantly running around town using Grant's name to open doors to lock up new bank loans to prop up his scheme. William Vanderbilt, son of Cornelius Vanderbilt, and the world's richest person at the time, loaned Grant $150,000 to help keep the company afloat. The next day Ward tried to get another $500,000 from Vanderbilt but this time was rebuffed.[11]

Grant thought all was well while this unfolded, until he approached his office one day and was met by an angry mob of investors demanding their money back. They informed the former president the bank that bared his name had failed. This was a stunning development and completely out of left field to the man who assumed he was succeeding wildly in his business affairs. Grant told a friend that day, "When I went downtown this morning I thought I was worth a great deal of money, now I don't know that I have $1; and probably my sons, too, have lost everything." His life savings were gone. Instead of being the millionaire he assumed was on paper, Grant and his wife were worth a total of around $210, combined.[12]

The financials showed the bank owed investors nearly $17 million against assets on the books worth just $69,000. It turns out Ward was simply cashing every investor check for his own personal use. Once he was in custody, Ward later admitted, "He [Grant] knew nothing. He took my word. He had the same information the customer had – and he had the same happiness, while it lasted." Ward claimed not a single victim of his scam ever bothered asking to see the government contracts he touted to investors. He gloated: "The were so pleased with the show of big profits that they were only too glad to have their apparent winnings pyramided." The stock market tanked in the aftermath of this calamity. Two other banks were forced to shut down, along with seven brokerages, from the collateral damage.[13]

Grant even lost the entire quarter of a million-dollar trust fund that had been set up for him when he left office. Ward used the money to invest in the bonds of a company that defaulted on their loans. The Grants were forced to scrounge for the basic necessities of life in old age. They accepted charity from friends. There was an immense outpouring of sympathy for the Civil War hero who remained America's most famous man. Grant was totally and utterly humiliated, admitting at the time, "I don't see how I can ever trust any human being again." Grant was so destitute that citizens began sending him money just so he could pay his bills. William Tecumseh Sherman, another architect of the Union's victory in the war, said his friend had "lost everything, and more in reputation."[14]

Less than a year later, Grant contracted a deadly form of throat cancer. The general had put off writing a book for many years but knew his days were numbered and wanted to leave his family some money before he was gone. So he finally took up writing a memoir, to be published by Mark Twain's publishing house. Grant finished his memoirs just one week before he died in 1885. The cancer in his throat was so painful he was forced to dictate much of the book to his wife in his final months. *The Personal Memoirs of U.S. Grant* is widely considered a masterpiece and one of the foremost military memoirs ever published. The book sold more than 300,000 copies of a two-volume set. It sold more copies in such a short period of time as any book up until that point in history. Grant's wife received almost half a million dollars from the book sales.

Grant was a man of honor. He refused to write about his own accomplishments, instead letting his actions speak for themselves in his memoir. Mark Twain was instrumental in getting the book published. Twain, who himself made a string of terrible investments over the course of his lifetime, later said, "It was the unimpeachable credit and respectability of Grant's name that enabled Fish and Ward to swindle the public. They could not have done it on their own reputations." Grant biographer Ron Chernow claims Grant was defeated in this endeavor by "his own fundamental decency." Grant was never a scammer himself, just supremely naive in his business dealings and his desire to get rich.

Don't Try to Get Rich Twice

The value of Ulysses S. Grant's trust fund ($250,000) and home in New York City ($100,000) when he got out of office would be the equivalent of millions of dollars today. While Grant never considered himself a wealthy man or a success in business, he was set up with a sizable stipend for his years after being in the top office in the land. His problem was he tried to take that money and multiply it. There's nothing wrong with investing, of course. In fact, most retirees need to continue investing their capital for growth in their later years because life spans continue to rise, meaning your money may need to last many decades into retirement. But there is a difference between prudent investing and speculation. Fred Schwed Jr., author of the wonderfully titled book *Where Are the Customers' Yachts* wrote, "Speculation is an effort, probably unsuccessful, to turn a little money into a lot. Investment is an effort, which should be successful, to prevent a lot of money from becoming a little."[15] Grant tried to get rich twice and lost everything.

Warren Buffett once gave a talk to a group of MBA students at the University of Maryland. One student asked the Oracle of Omaha to name some common errors successful people make with their money. Buffett told the class, "Anyone who has become rich twice is dumb. Why would you risk what you need and have for what you don't need? If you are already rich, there is no upside to taking on a lot more risk, but there is disgrace on the downside."[16] Obviously, being rich is a good problem to have, but there are a host of lessons we can learn from the myriad of successful people who have struck out in their financial lives or gotten caught up in a fraud of epic proportions. Most of the people who lose big or get scammed out of their money tend to blame extenuating circumstances. Grant was a man of honor and never blamed anyone but himself, but he failed to realize how a single mistake can destroy your wealth if it's a big enough miscalculation. Just one wrong move and, poof, it's all gone.

You only have to invest all your money in something you don't understand ONCE to see it all vanish. You only have to turn your life savings over to a charlatan or huckster ONCE to see them bleed you dry. You only have to become overconfident in your investment skills ONCE to see a concentrated position completely go against you. You only have to place your trust in the wrong individual or organization ONCE to ruin your financial future.

But the flipside of this is true as well.

You only have to learn how to manage your money ONCE to preserve your hard-earned savings. You only have to come up with a solid business idea ONCE to create a powerful stream of income.

You only have to get lucky ONCE to see your career, earnings, or business opportunities take off. You only have to get your financial affairs in order ONCE to begin seeing meaningful results.

Most people will never become a household name, create a sustainable business venture, or strike it rich on a transformative business idea. But everyone can control their own personal finances by making intelligent spending and saving decisions with their money. If you never learn the ins and outs of money management and financial decision-making it doesn't matter how many times you get lucky. Eventually your luck will run out. There are a million and one ways to become wealthy but only a few simple ways to stay wealthy. And because wealth is always relative to your past situation, these ideas hold no matter how much money you have. Most people don't become rich even ONCE but that doesn't mean you can't improve your lot in life by creating an intelligent financial plan and making better money decisions. Here are some ways to do this, regardless of your level of success in the political or business arenas:

> **Diversify your money and your life.** There's an old saying that you should concentrate your investments to get rich but diversify to stay rich. This may be true for the most successful of businesspeople and investors, but the statement also reeks of survivorship bias.
>
> Nearly every success story is accompanied by a lucky break. Apple got bailed out by a loan from Microsoft in the late 1990s. Without it they may not have become one of the largest publicly traded companies in the world. Coca-Cola was created when someone accidentally added carbonation to medicinal syrup. Play Doh was originally supposed to be a wallpaper cleaner. Toothpaste didn't take off as a regularly used product until someone added bubbles so people could get the sensation that it was actually doing something to their mouth.
>
> Diversification is important for people at any level of wealth. Peter Bernstein once said, "Diversification is the only rational deployment of our ignorance." That includes investments as well as your career path. If you put all your human capital into one venture it can leave you exposed to the vagaries of consumer tastes, the economy, bad timing, or simply bad luck. It's not just financial frauds that can take you down when you fail to diversify your money and business interests.

Figure out your level of enough. After leaving office, Grant felt he deserved to become a millionaire to have his money match his status in the pecking order. The crazy thing is Grant had something money can't buy – the respect of the country and the world at large. Every business owner and investor on the planet craved the respect and admiration Grant had received from the public but he just didn't know when to say enough is enough when it came to his finances. *The Chronicle of Philanthropy* performed a study where they asked people who inherited money, "What amount of money would you need to feel totally secure?" No matter how much they inherited or how much they already had, the number people named was always roughly twice what they inherited.[17]

Berkshire Hathaway Vice Chairman Charlie Munger once said, "There's an old saying, 'What good is envy? It's the one sin you can't have any fun at.' It's 100% destructive. Resentment is crazy. Revenge is crazy. Envy is crazy. If you get those things out of your life early, life works a lot better." Unfortunately, there will always be someone making more money or receiving more accolades or earning a better job title or wielding more power than you. You don't have to look very hard to feel insignificant these days, what with the advent of humble-bragging and fake lives on social media platforms and the like.

There's nothing wrong with looking to better yourself in life. One of the biggest reasons we've experienced so much progress over the past few hundred years is that it's part of the human condition to wake up in the morning and want to better your position in life. But people who don't know when enough is enough can find themselves in trouble when trying to keep up with the Joneses. In the race of life, you're not competing with your peers, co-workers, friends, or social media stars. You're competing with yourself, or better yet, prior versions of yourself. This is especially true when it comes to finding contentment in money matters. Richard Carlson (no relation) once wrote, "It's not that having a lot of things is bad, wrong, or harmful in and of itself, only that the desire to have more and more and more is insatiable. As long as you think more is better, you'll never be satisfied."[18]

When you have no idea how much money is enough for you, the simple answer will always be in search of more.

Notes

1. Murray N. *Simple Wealth, Inevitable Wealth: How You and Your Financial Advisor Can Grow Your Fortune in Stock Mutual Funds.* Southold, NY: The Nick Murray Company, Inc.; 1999.
2. Rosenberg Y. The super-rich are just as miserable as the rest of us. *The Week* [Internet]. 2014 Nov 4. Available from: https://theweek.com/articles/442718/superrich-are-just-miserable-rest
3. Pinsker J. The reason many ultrarich people aren't satisfied with their wealth. *The Atlantic* [Internet]. 2018 Dec 4. Available from: https://www.theatlantic.com/family/archive/2018/12/rich-people-happy-money/577231/
4. Rank SM. Getting to know the other side of General Grant. History on the Net [Internet] Available from: https://www.historyonthenet.com/getting-to-know-general-grant
5. Schmidgall G. *Intimate with Walt: Whitman's Conversations with Horace Traubel, 1882–92.* Iowa City: University of Iowa Press; 2001.
6. Twain M. *Mark Twain in Eruption: Hitherto Unpublished Pages about Men and Events.* New York: Harper; 1940.
7. Chernow R. Grant. New York: Penguin Random House; 2017.
8. Ibid.
9. Ibid.
10. Ibid.
11. Ibid.
12. Ibid.
13. Ibid.
14. Ibid.
15. Schwed F. *Where Are the Customers' Yachts? Or a Good Hard Look at Wall Street.* Hoboken, New Jersey: John Wiley & Sons; 2006.
16. Kass D. Commentary on Warren Bufffett and Berkshire Hathaway: Warren Buffett's meeting with University of Maryland MBA/MS students. University of Maryland Robert H. Smith School of Business [Internet]. 2016 Nov 18. Available from: http://blogs.rhsmith.umd.edu/david-kass/uncategorized/warren-buffetts-meeting-with-university-of-maryland-mbams-students-november-18-2016/
17. McVeig S. What it's like to grow up with more money than you'll ever spent. The Cut [Internet]. 2019 Mar 28. Available from: https://www.thecut.com/2019/03/abigail-disney-has-more-money-than-shell-ever-spend.html
18. Carlson R. *Don't Sweat the Small Stuff ... And It's All Small Stuff: Simple Ways to Keep the Little Things from Taking Over Your Life.* New York: Hyperion; 1997.

CHAPTER

7

When Fraud Flourishes

When the cash value of promises goes up, when tomorrows are being sold early, swindlers are among the first to profit.

–Jonathan Kwity

If you've been paying attention so far, you'll notice a lot of similarities among the hustlers, scammers, and environments in which frauds tend to occur. Every fraud is unique in its own right because the circumstances are always different, but there are themes we can point to that show the conditions that tend to be present when fraud truly flourishes.

When There's an 'Expert' with a Good Story

Jerry Seinfeld once observed, "It's amazing that the amount of news that happens in the world every day always just exactly fits the newspaper." Author Michael Crichton once said in a speech that the media often carries a credibility it doesn't deserve. He called this the Gell-Mann Amnesia effect, named for Nobel Prize-winning physicist Murray Gell-Mann, with whom he discussed this idea. Crichton explains this effect as follows:

> Briefly stated, the Gell-Mann Amnesia effect is as follows. You open the newspaper to an article on some subject you know well.

71

In Murray's case, physics. In mine, show business. You read the article and see the journalist has absolutely no understanding of either the facts or the issues. Often, the article is so wrong it actually presents the story backward – reversing cause and effect. I call these the "wet streets cause rain" stories. Paper's full of them.

In any case, you read with exasperation or amusement the multiple errors in a story, and then turn the page to national or international affairs, and read as if the rest of the newspaper was somehow more accurate about Palestine than the baloney you just read. You turn the page, and forget what you know.

This line of thinking follows for financial "experts" as well. It's easy to spot someone in our own lives who embellishes or constantly lies to us but when it comes to our finances we simply trust the first intelligent-sounding person wearing a bow tie. If someone sounds like they know what they're talking about, makes a lot of promises, or uses jargon you don't understand, then they must know what they're doing, right? Au contraire.

We are storytelling creatures, and the scam artists who push people into frauds or scams are masters at spinning a yarn. One of the unfortunate realities of the investment business is that, all else equal, a talented sales staff will trump a talented investment staff when attracting capital from investors. And that's in the legitimate money management business. When it comes to scammers and fraudsters, all bets are off. And in many cases, these people are better at sales and marketing than even the best and brightest on Wall Street.

Crichton also relayed an anecdote that explains how things typically work when so-called experts over-promise and under-deliver. There's an old joke in which a child comes down on Christmas morning and finds the room around the tree filled with horse excrement. When the boy jumps up and down for joy, his parents ask why he's so happy at the sight of a room filled with horse manure. The boy replies, "With this much horsesh*t, there must be a pony."[1]

The old there-must-be-a-pony effect is essential to the proliferation of financial fraud and malfeasance. Unfortunately, most financial promises attached to a good story don't come with a pony either, but they are full of horsesh*t.

When Greed Is Abundant

In his classic *Manias, Panics, and Crashes,* Charles Kindelberger outlines the five phases of a bubble:

> *Phase One: Displacement.* An event or innovation occurs that sharply changes expectations. This phase is typically grounded in reality and good intentions.
>
> *Phase Two: Expansion.* This is the stage where the narrative takes hold and people begin bidding up asset prices.
>
> *Phase Three: Euphoria.* By this point, all bets are off. Everyone assumes they can get rich easily and very quickly. Risk is taken with abandon and nobody worries about the hangover in the morning. During the dot-com bubble, this is the point where people decided they could make more money day trading IPOs than going to their day job. Euphoria makes people think the good times will last forever, or at the very least, they won't be the ones holding the bag when it turns.
>
> *Phase Four: Crisis.* The inevitable other side of any boom is a bust. This is the phase where the insiders begin selling, and panic buying quickly shifts to panic selling.
>
> *Phase Five: Contagion.* Just as prices overshoot to the upside from euphoria, they often overshoot to the downside once the contagion of bad news spreads and people think things will never get better again.[2]

Phase three is the lynchpin in this entire cycle, because without greed, there is no fear. Without a bubble, there is no bust. And without greed and bubbles there isn't nearly as much fraud taking place.

Gordon Gekko, as played by Michael Douglas in the classic movie *Wall Street,* said, "The point is, ladies and gentleman, that greed, for lack of a better word, is good. Greed is right, greed works. Greed clarifies, cuts through, and captures the essence of the evolutionary spirit. Greed, in all of its forms; greed for life, for money, for love, knowledge has marked the upward surge of mankind."

This quote actually isn't as far out there as some make it out to be. Gekko makes some valid points. The problem is we humans *always* take things too far, so once greed infects a market there's no reining it in. The cycle goes something like this:

- After markets crash, they begin to rise when the economic or corporate landscape shifts from catastrophic to just terrible, because markets are more about relative (better or worse) than absolute (good or bad) news. These are the rallies no one trusts because people still see the carnage all around them from the market or economic downturn.

- Eventually other investors begin to take notice of rising markets that aren't rolling over. Rising prices attract buyers just as falling prices attract sellers, so higher asset prices become something of a self-fulfilling prophecy as they continue to push higher (for a time).
- After markets have risen for long enough that people see their neighbors getting rich or read about others making money in the *Wall Street Journal* the herd mentality kicks in and greed takes over. Rinse and repeat.

Bull markets make us believe we're invincible just as bear markets make us feel like idiots. The truth is usually somewhere in-between in both scenarios, but those feelings of invincibility can lead to a lax decision-making process when it comes to choosing the right people to work with.

It's during this greed phase of the market cycle that investors become easy marks for scammers. Greed clouds your vision as it becomes harder to come by easy profits. As those easy profits dissipate, people are willing to take more risk to earn rewards they feel they're now entitled to. So people reach for investments or strategies they shouldn't because they begin to believe the market owes them something. This scenario is a huckster's dream because they don't even need to try very hard to take advantage of their unsuspecting victims.

Joseph "Yellow Kid" Weil was one of the most successful con men of the early 1900s, employing a variety of scams to bilk people out of their money: fake merchandise; a dog swindle where he pretended to have rare, expensive breed of dog for sale; staging fake prize fights; and selling land that didn't belong to him. It's estimated he made out with $3 to $8 million over the course of a 40-year career as a con artist. Towards the end of his life Weil admitted, "Men like myself could not have existed without the victim's' covetous, criminal greed."[3]

When Capital Becomes Blind

Walter Bagehot was an early editor at *The Economist* in the mid-to-late nineteenth century. In a collection of his essays, he wrote about what happens when a moment of insanity strikes and capital turns blind to risks:

> At intervals, from causes which are not to the present purpose, the money of these people – the blind capital (as we call it) of the country – is particularly large and craving; it seeks for someone to devour it, and there is "plethora" – it finds someone, and there is "speculation" – it is devoured, and there is "panic."[4]

Charlatans and scam artists understand this dynamic better than most, and you can bet when capital becomes blind they will be there waiting to pounce. Sometimes capital turns blind because you have so much of it you simply let your guard down.

That's exactly what happened to The King, Elvis Presley. At the tail end of his career, Elvis owned a private plane he rarely used so his father, Vernon, decided to help by putting it up for sale. An experienced con artist by the name of Fred Pro swooped in and hatched an elaborate scam to take not only the plane, but also some of Elvis's money. To get a foot in the door, Pro concocted a detailed résumé which showed him to be a veteran of the airline industry. Once he gained their trust, the con man's plan involved that involved buying the plane, paying off the remaining loan Elvis owed, then leasing the plane back to himself, thus netting The King a cool monthly profit of $1,000/month on the deal. Pro said he planned on making up for his losses by chartering the plane as a pilot.

Pro took the plane for a test flight all the way to New York City, using the plane itself as collateral to secure a $1 million loan. There was just one more thing he needed from Elvis to close the deal – the $340,000 check, which was how much equity Elvis has in the plane, to be used for upgrades on the aircraft. Those upgrades never took place because Pro never planned on actually leasing out the private plane. Instead, he absconded with the $340,000 and wouldn't you know it, every single one of his checks bounced. Yet he and his other con artist friends flew all around the country in what was basically a free private jet for months, until they read in the paper Elvis had died. At that point, Pro assumed he would own it free and clear, but Vernon Presley finally went to the authorities when he figured out he'd been defrauded.

Vernon told the FBI, "You know I got to thinking. Maybe that this guy, the reason he was wanting upgrading money was to use it himself, not to – this might have been a planned deal all the way through."[5]

Um...ya think?

Pro's plan all along was to blind the Presleys with a deal that was too good to pass up. They were so swayed by the idea they could earn a profit on the deal that they failed to perform any due diligence on their buyer other than what he told them.

Legendary mutual fund manager Peter Lynch once said, "Spend at least as much time researching a stock as you would choosing a refrigerator." The idea here is that people often spend more time debating the merits of a minor money decision than they do one that will potentially impact them for years to come. There's nothing wrong with using extra care and attention when making a big financial decision. Unfortunately, when capital becomes blind, we often throw caution to the wind, and that can lead to people getting taken advantage of.

When the Banking Industry Gets Involved

Steve Eisman is one of the most memorable characters to come out of the best book written about the Great Financial Crisis, Michael Lewis's *The Big Short* (Eisman was played by Steve Carell in the movie adaptation). After learning about the cascading problems subprime loans were causing the financial system, Eisman and his team began shorting Wall Street bank stocks such as Bank of America, UBS, Citigroup, and Lehman Brothers, betting these companies would take a hit for all the subprime debt they held on their balance sheets. Eisman also shorted the now defunct firm Merrill Lynch, which was later bought by Bank of America. When asked why he shorted Merrill, Eisman replied, "We have a simple thesis. There is going to be a calamity, and whenever there is a calamity, Merrill is there." Michael Lewis continued on this thought:

> When it came time to bankrupt Orange County with bad advice, Merrill was there. When the Internet went bust, Merrill was there. Way back in the 1980s, when the first bond trader was let off his leash and lost hundreds of millions of dollars, Merrill was there to take the hit. That was Eisman's logic: the logic of Wall Street's pecking order. Goldman Sachs was the big kid who ran the games in this neighborhood. Merrill Lynch was the little fat kid assigned the least pleasant roles, just happy to be a part of

things. The game, as Eisman saw it, was crack the whip. He assumed Merrill Lynch had taken its assigned place at the end of the chain.[6]

Eisman was right, of course, as all these bank stocks got destroyed in the crisis, but it's not so much that Merrill Lynch played a role in all of these past crises as it is Wall Street circling when there's blood in the water. Banks have a nasty habit of fanning the flames when markets take off because no one wants to be left behind on Wall Street when there's money to be made off Main Street. And when people are making money there is sure to be fraud involved somewhere along the way. During the housing mania, the FBI reported mortgage-related fraud was up fivefold from 2000 to 2006.

Household Finance Corporation was founded in the 1870s, but during the real estate bubble of the aughts, the company was making loans at its fastest pace ever. The source of their growth was coming from second mortgages with an odd sales tactic. They were offering 15-year fixed-rate mortgage loans to people looking to pull money out of their homes in a rising housing market. But they disguised these 15-year loans as 30-year loans to prospective clients, showing them what their payment stream would look like spread out over a three-decade period. The borrower was told this made the interest rate 7% but the effective rate was actually 12.5%. This was blatant fraud and many borrowers realized what happened when a reporter began looking into the company's sales tactics. Household was forced to pay a fine in a class action lawsuit but was sold to another bank shortly thereafter.[7]

Wall Street firms aren't always perpetrators of fraud, but you better believe they will be there waiting to take advantage when markets reach a fever pitch. And even if the banks keep everything completely above board, there will be other firms pushed to the brink of fraud to keep up. You can take that to the bank (pun intended).

When Individuals Begin Taking Their Cues from the Crowd

Going to the grocery store can be tricky because I have three young children. So, I buy *a lot* of stuff from Amazon in terms of food and household goods to save on trips to the store. Jeff Bezos has me trained well enough that Amazon is almost always the first place I look for an item we need around the house. Whenever I buy something new, I almost always choose the one marked 'Amazon's Choice' if I don't have a specific brand in mind. This may seem irrational on my part but when people don't know exactly how to react or make certain decisions, we look to others to figure out what the correct behavior should be.

This is why so many of your favorite network sitcoms use a fake laugh track for every single joke whether it's good, bad, or otherwise. It turns out that research shows audiences laugh longer and more often when a laugh track follows a joke, no matter how corny or overused it is. Audiences also rate the material as being funnier, which is even more effective for the worst jokes. We often look to others to decide how to react during certain situations because we are status-seeking creatures and no one wants to be left out of the joke (even when it's not funny).

Robert Cialdini calls this weapon of influence the principle of social proof. Social proof is the idea that actions are seen as more appropriate when others are doing it. This is a double-edged sword because following the crowd can be a useful life hack under certain situations, like knowing where to pay at a store you've never been to by simply finding the line of other people waiting to pay. But using shortcuts when it comes to your finances can leave you vulnerable to those willing and eager to take advantage of the herd mentality. One of the reasons fraud tends to spread like a virus is because it's difficult to witness others earn what looks like easy profits.

In the early 1900s, Oscar Hartzell conned some 70,000 people in the Midwest through promises of a 5,000% return on their money. Hartzell used a scheme similar to the Nigerian Prince scam wherein he promised access to billions of dollars from an inheritance for Sir Francis Drake, a pirate who supposedly looted a fortune from Spanish ships in the 1500s. The story was completely made up and it turns out Hartzell's mother had fallen for the con, which gave her son the idea to try it on others. Farmers from all over the Midwest fell for Hartzell's story. And when the authorities tried to shut it down, they received thousands of letters from angry citizens who were worried the attorney general in Iowa would derail their dreams of millions from a long-lost inheritance. So many people believed the money existed that everyone who handed money to Hartzell to help him get the inheritance from England to the US had no other choice but to believe.

John Kenneth Galbraith once wrote, "Perhaps, indeed, there is opportunity. Maybe there *is* that treasure on the floor of the Red Sea. A rich history provides proof, however, as often or more often, there is only delusion and self-delusion." Even Hartzell himself fell for his own made up story, repeatedly ranting in jail that his claims were true after authorities finally put an end to his scam.

When Markets Are Rocking

When things are really good or really bad it makes for fertile breeding ground for fraud. Market booms and busts toy with our emotions but in different ways. It's typically the booms more so than busts that suck more people into forms of financial fraud. No one wants to feel left out when everyone around them is making money. So, when things are going well, risk management goes out the window, people become more lax about their due diligence procedures, and everyone becomes more trusting in money-making ventures.

For every bust there must first be a boom, and the boom that preceded the Great Depression was the roaring 20s. The 1920s introduced innovation the likes of which the mass consumer had never experienced before. People were introduced to several luxuries we now take for granted – radios, refrigerators, washing machines, irons, full electricity in their homes, private indoor toilets, central heating, air conditioning, automobiles and much more. And the innovation that allowed so many people to make these upgrades in their lives was the explosive growth of consumer borrowing during this time. People were purchasing items on credit en masse for the first time in history.

The stock market boomed as it never had before. The ensuing market crash unwound the boom and more. Frederick Lewis Allen's book *Only Yesterday: An Informal History of the 1920s* captured the sentiment of this boom, and its aftermath, beautifully:

> Prosperity is more than an economic condition: it is a state of mind. The Big Bull Markets had been more than the climax of the business cycle; it had been the climax of a cycle in American mass thinking and mass emotion. There was hardly a man or woman in the country whose attitude toward life had not been affected by it in some degree and was not now affected by the sudden and brutal shattering of hope. With the Big Bull Market gone and prosperity going, Americans were soon to find themselves

living in an altered world which called for new adjustments, new ideas, new habits of thought, and a new order of values. The psychological climate was changing; the ever-shifting currents of American life were turning into new channels.[8]

In many ways, financial fraud is also a state of mind for both those peddling it and those on the receiving end of being scammed.

When the Opportunity Presents Itself

There are a number of reasons for fraudulent behavior. Sometimes people are simply lifelong con artists who defraud others because they've perfected the game, it gives them a thrill, and it can make them wealthy. Others scam people out of money through an internal justification by rationalizing their actions. These situations usually start out as a legitimate idea but morph into fraud when that idea needs to be taken to the next level to succeed. Then there are the cases where people are motivated to commit fraud because of perverse incentives or some perceived financial need or desire.

But all of these situations require one thing to take place – opportunity. Without an opening, without greedy victims, without an ineffective system, without the requisite lack of controls in place, without an opportunity to take advantage of people, fraud never gets off the ground. And sometimes that opportunity presents itself in crazy ways.

Two brothers from a small town in Spain purchased what they thought was a painting by Francisco Goya, a Spanish painter from the late-eighteenth and early-nineteenth century. But after putting down a deposit for the painting the brothers quickly realized they'd been swindled when the certificate of authenticity never arrived. The case went to trial, where an expert determined the painting was in fact a fake, relieving the brothers of the remaining debt they owed on the deal.

The brothers learned a lesson after this ordeal, but it wasn't necessarily the one most would assume. Instead of learning from their mistake, they tried to see if they could make others fall for the same scam they fell for. In 2014, the brothers tried to sell their forged painting to an Arab sheik for a down payment of 1.7 million Swiss francs. Not only did they try to sell the same fake painting they had been duped into buying, but they did so at an even higher price than they bought it for! Apparently even the forged art market has pretty decent returns. Alas, there was yet *another* forgery involved with this scam, but this time it wasn't a painting. When they tried to cash their deposit for the painting, it was determined the money was forged. And the worst part of it all is that they were charged a commission of 300,000 euros to enter into the deal. Both the sheik and the intermediary who accepted the commission were nowhere to be found once it was discovered the currency was fake.[9]

Not everyone would have gone down the same path if given the opportunity. But there are people who seem like generally decent humans who end up committing fraud simply because it seems like it's there for the taking.

When Human Beings Are Involved

Reminiscences of a Stock Operator was originally published in 1923 by Edwin Lefevre. He wrote, "There is nothing new in Wall Street. There can't be because speculation is as old as the hills. Whatever happens in the stock market today has happened before and will happen again." Substitute 'fraud' for 'stock market' in that sentence and it still rings true.

J.H. Kelly insisted he could perform medical miracles through a "practical scientific system." This system involved Kelly helping sick people clear their minds of all problems to concentrate hard enough to "think it away." As preposterous as this sounds, Kelly became a millionaire many times over. By the year 1900, he was receiving thousands of letters a day from people looking for his healing touch. He charged anywhere from $1,000 to $1,600 in which he would send people a postcard giving them an exact day and time to clear their brain and thus be cured of whatever ailed them.[10]

Jude Devereux became a best-selling romance novelist who has 30 or so books on the *New York Times* bestseller list. The sale of her books made her a millionaire many times over which made her a perfect mark for a financial scam. After losing a son to an accident and going through a divorce, a psychic preyed on Devereux at a weak moment in her life. This psychic, who used a fake name, told the author money would attract evil if it remained in her bank account. Deveraux handed over an estimated $17 million. When she testified at the trial for her scam artist psychic, Deveraux admitted, "When I look back on it now, it was outrageous. I was out of my mind."[11]

Markets, economies, regulations, and technology are constantly changing and adapting, but human nature remains the one constant throughout history. As long as humans walk the earth, there will be people who take advantage of that human nature and there will *always* be people who get taken advantage of.

When Innovation Runs Rampant

Times of great technological change provide an ideal atmosphere for financial fraud. It's during these times of transition where you hear terms like "paradigm shift" that people begin to lose touch with reality when it comes to their finances. Everyone would like to believe fast change will lead to quick profits, which is why scam artists thrive during financial booms, political upheaval, technological innovation, and times of transition. These times bring about great hope but also great uncertainty about the future. Hope is never a good investment strategy, but it makes for a wonderful sales tactic. We all love to dream about becoming healthier and wealthier, and it's never easier to sell these dreams than when people are filled with optimism about what the future holds.

During times of great change, we perceive conditions as being less risky, hence people are more willing to take risks with their money because they feel it's actually a safer environment to invest. Technological innovation has improved the world in countless ways, but those periods of transition can make it difficult for people to gauge risk. When antilock brakes were installed on cars people simply drove more aggressively. When commercial ships adopted radar technology it was assumed there would be fewer collisions on the seas. Instead, the captains drove more recklessly.[12]

In the next chapter, we'll look at how advances in technology can have simultaneously positive and negative consequences depending on the time horizon.

Notes

1. Crichton M. Why speculate? The Great Ideas Online No. 332. [Internet]. 2005 Jul. Available from: http://larvatus.com/michael-crichton-why-speculate/

2. Kindelberger CP and Aliber R. *Manias, Panics, and Crashes: A History of Financial Crises.* Hoboken, New Jersey: John Wiley & Sons; 2000.

3. Nash JR. *Hustlers and Con Men: An Anecdotal History of the Confidence Man and His Games.* New York: M. Evans & Company; 1976.

4. Bagehot W. The works and life of Walter Bagehot, ed. Mrs. Russell Barrington. The Works in Nine Volumes. Vol. 2. London: Longmans, Green, and Co.; 1915. Available from: https://oll.libertyfund.org/titles/bagehot-the-works-and-life-of-walter-bagehot-vol-2-historical-financial-essays

5. Howard D. *Chasing Phil: The Adventures of Two Undercover Agents with the World's Most Charming Con Man.* New York: Random House; 2017.

6. Lewis M. *The Big Short: Inside the Doomsday Machine.* New York: W. W. Norton & Company; 2010.

7. Ibid.

8. Allen FL. *Only Yesterday: An Informal History of The 1920s.* New York: Harper & Row; 1931.

9. Escofet JM. Art swindlers selling fake Goya get paid in photocopied bills. El País. [Internet] 2015 Feb 20. Available from: https://elpais.com/elpais/2015/02/20/inenglish/1424447006_201514.html

10. Nash JR. *Hustlers and Con Men: An Anecdotal History of the Confidence Man and His Games.* New York: M. Evans & Company; 1976.

11. Romance novelist testifies that she handed over $1million to psychic 'who promised to store cash at St Patrick's Cathedral in return for giving writer a peaceful divorce.' Mail Online [Internet]. 2013 Sep 11. Available from: https://www.dailymail.co.uk/news/article-2416972/Bestselling-author-Jude-Deveraux-testifies-scammed-fortune-tellers.html

12. Gonzales L. *Deep Survival: Who Lives, Who Dies and Why.* New York: W.W. Norton & Company; 2003.

CHAPTER

The Siren Song of New Technologies

Gold rushes tend to encourage impetuous investments. A few will pay off, but when the frenzy is behind us, we will look back incredulously at the wreckage of failed ventures and wonder, 'Who funded those companies? What was going on in their minds? Was that just a mania at work?'

—Bill Gates

Glass was created millions of years ago when a comet struck the planet and emitted enough heat to create a chemical reaction that turned silicon dioxide into a liquid that changed into a solid as it cooled. But glass didn't serve much of a purpose until another invention brought it to life. Johannes Gutenberg's printing press led people across Europe to realize they were farsighted when they tried to read. Demand for reading glasses skyrocketed. This increase in demand led to a wave of innovation in other areas as scientists began to experiment with different lenses.

Lens experimentation led to the microscope, which literally opened our eyes to the inner workings of cells in the body. Then in the 1970s, researchers at Corning Glassworks developed an astonishingly clear type of glass. Scientists at Bell Labs took the fibers from that glass and sent laser beams down the length of the fibers using optical signals, which worked much like computer coding with zeroes and ones. Mashing these seemingly unrelated inventions together – clear glass with fibers and lasers – created what is now known as fiber optics. It turns out fiber optics are extremely efficient at sending electrical signals at a greater bandwidth than other cables. This efficiency makes fiber optic cables better at sending signals over long distances than the original copper cables used in the past. The Atlantic Ocean has ten different fiber optic cables which easily carry the bulk of our data and voice communications around the globe instantaneously. The cables are so efficient at handling signals that you could take all the voice and data traffic going back and forth between North America and Europe and hold it in the palm of your hand.[1]

And it just so happens that this little thing called the Internet eventually came along, which required greater bandwidth that fiber optic cables could provide. So glass is now being used to transmit the information we consume every day on the little glass supercomputers we carry around in our pockets for work, play, entertainment, socializing, and wasting time. It's highly likely that the infrastructure for this system would have taken a lot longer to put in place if it wasn't for the dot-com bubble of the 1990s.

Bubbles evoke all sorts of stories about the madness of crowds and the eventual pain that follows during the inevitable crash. The dot-com bubble certainly led to plenty of madness and eventual losses as speculators tried to make sense of how far technological innovation could take things in what was being touted as the "New Economy." Intel, Cisco, Microsoft, and Oracle, some of the biggest tech darlings of the 1990s, were worth a combined $83 billion at the outset of 1995. Just five short years later, as the tech bubble inflated to astronomical levels, this group had grown to a combined market cap of nearly $2 trillion! That was a gain of well over 2,100%, or 80% per year for five years. In 1999 alone 13 tech stocks were up 1,000% or more, including the biggest winner of them all, Qualcomm, which rose an astonishing 2,700%. Amazon was up 966% a year earlier.[2]

The bubble finally popped in early-2000 when investors realized the fundamentals of these businesses couldn't possibly live up to the insane growth priced into their share prices. Amazon was down close to 95%. Apple fell almost 80% in value while Cisco (down 86%), Intel (down 78%), Oracle (down 84%), Qualcomm (down 83%), and Microsoft (down 60%) all suffered similarly huge losses. Plenty

Table 8.1   Tech Stock Losses during the Dot-Com Crash

Company	Stock Losses in the Dot-Com Crash
Amazon (AMZN)	-95%
Apple (AAPL)	-80%
Cisco (CSCO)	-86%
Intel (INTL)	-78%
Oracle (ORCL)	-83%
Microsoft (MSFT)	-60%

of other stocks that went public in the 1990s completely went out of business, including the infamous Pets.com.

The outcome of this rollercoaster wasn't all bad though. Too much competition for investment, overcapacity, and lofty expectations during a bubble can lead to enormous losses for those left holding the bag when the bubble eventually pops. But if some of that investment is used for productive purposes, it can lead to net gains for society when it's put to use. Before the dot-com bubble popped, telecom companies raised almost $2 trillion in equity and $600 billion in debt from investors eager to bet on the future. These companies laid down more than 80 million miles of fiber optic cables, which represented more than three-quarters of all digital wiring installed in the US up to that point in all of history. There was so much overcapacity from this build-out that 85% of these fiber optic cables were still unused as of late-2005. And within four years of the end of the dot-com bubble, the cost of bandwidth had fallen by 90%. So despite more people coming online by the day during this period, costs fell and there was so much capacity available that those who were left standing were able to build out the Internet as we know it today.[3]

Before trains can travel, you need to lay the tracks, which is a perfect segue into our next charlatan, George Hudson, and his role in the railway bubble of the nineteenth century.

The Railway Napoleon

Technological innovation isn't a prerequisite for fraud to occur, but it sure makes it a whole lot easier. Innovation breeds change, change breeds emotion, and emotion adds fuel to the fire when money is involved. There's a reason financial bubbles are often called manias – they elicit heightened levels of energy, excitement, and activity. Hucksters are drawn to financial manias like a millennial to avocado toast because it's easier to deceive people when they think humanity is entering a "new era" or "paradigm shift." Self-promoters take their hubris to another level to prey on the greed of others during these times. George Hudson saw the British railway bubble of the mid-nineteenth century as an opportune time to profit from the excitement in the air. There was a wave of innovation taking place, and the emotions of the crowd who were looking to get rich quickly led to one of the more underrated historical bubbles on record.

Like most bubbles, the railway mania actually started out as a good idea that was simply taken too far by investors and those selling railway projects alike. The first commuter trains appeared in the United Kingdom during the 1820s. They traveled just 12.5 miles per hour, which reduced the trip from London to Glasgow to 24 hours. The *Railway Times* asked, without even a hint of sarcasm, "What more could any reasonable man want?"[4] The first railway mania hit in 1825 with the opening of the first steam railway. An economic downturn snuffed out any speculation and by 1840, shares of the main railway companies were selling at a discount to their issue price (stocks acted more like bonds than stocks back then). There were 2,000 miles of track completed at this point, which led some to speculate whether the national railway system in Britain was already finished.[5]

Memories are short when people think there's money to be made so this first mini-mania in railway stocks became a distant memory by the summer of 1842. That's when Prince Albert of the Royal Family persuaded Queen Victoria to take her first train ride. That was the all-clear investors needed to hop aboard the train that was railway stocks. By 1844, investors viewed railway stocks as safe and secure with huge upside potential. It didn't take long for that cautious optimism to morph into reckless speculation.[6]

George Hudson was one of the original modern capitalists, using publicity, salesmanship, and a cult of personality to attract enormous amounts of capital and goodwill from the public. Best described by his contemporaries as energetic, abrasive, bullying, penny-pinching, rule-bending, and overweight, Hudson was a shrewd businessman who knew how to persuade people to do what was best for him and his companies.[7] Innovation helped trains travel farther distances and carry heavier loads, so Hudson pounced on the opportunity by creating his own line of railways in the 1830s. Through a series of consolidations, mergers, schemes, bribes, acquisitions, and an uncanny ability to sell, his railways consolidated more power than any other in the railway industry, eventually creating the largest railway company in Britain. By 1844, Hudson oversaw one-third of the total tracks in operation, measuring over 1,000 miles in distance, quickly becoming chairman for a number of railway companies.[8]

Company heads were not paid the astronomical sums CEOs can earn today, so Hudson became frustrated with how little he was getting paid for his work. So he decided to use his position of influence to make things happen on his own. Auditing was basically nonexistent at the time, which allowed Hudson and his directors to go nuts. And even if they wanted to challenge Hudson, none of the other directors had his level of knowledge or salesmanship. Not content to rest on his laurels or his morals, Hudson ruled with an iron fist. His M.O. was to act in complete secrecy by keeping his fellow directors and shareholders in the dark about the inner workings of his companies. This included a refusal to hold finance meetings, changes to accounting methods, and general obfuscation of the financial statements of the corporations he led. When Hudson joined the board of one railway company in 1842, his first order of business was announcing an immediate change to the company's accounting methods, proclaiming, "I will have no statistics on my railway!"[9] This is an obvious red flag, but when people are making money and change is afoot few pay any heed to red flags.

Nearly 500 new railway companies were in existence by the summer of 1845, with stock prices in the sector up a cool 500%. As share prices rose during the 1840s so too did Hudson's bank account. The palatial estate he purchased at the entrance to Hyde Park was the largest private home in all of London. Hudson became synonymous with business success as the mere mention of his name by promoters provided enough credibility for the sale of stock on a new railway project. Hudson quickly became one of the most prominent figures in the social and political class of Great Britain in the nineteenth century through a combination of wealth, fame, and charisma.[10]

Although he was skilled at selling, Hudson didn't exactly have to twist anyone's arm to invest in these new projects. Money was flowing in faster than Usain Bolt with the wind at his back. Investors of all shapes and sizes were basically throwing money at Hudson-backed railway projects, as optimism about the future of travel reached a fever pitch. By June 1945 the Board of Trade was considering over 8,000 miles of new railway, which was 4 times more than the existing system and almost 20 times the length of England. There were literally blueprints for tracks that started nowhere and went nowhere with no planned stops along the way. The estimated cost of the nearly 1,200 railways under consideration was more than £560 million. To put this number in perspective, that was more than the national income of the entire country![11]

The most mind-boggling aspect of all this money pouring in is that the source of capital was almost entirely private investors. This wasn't the government investing in the infrastructure of their country but investors who were looking to get rich. As the railway bubble grew in size from overinvestment, Hudson's self-control loosened. They even nicknamed him the 'Railway Napoleon' for his grandiose ideas and centralized decision-making process. To attract investors the railway companies offered fat dividend payments. The companies he ran were also known to see suspicious spikes in price the day before a takeover announcement, a clear sign of insider trading by Hudson and his fellow directors who had the knowledge in advance.[12] This bubble also contained an accelerant in the form of a growing media presence.

The Media's Role in a Bubble

Technological innovation not only makes people feel better about the prospects for the future, but it makes it easier for others to learn about what's going on around them. Better access to news and information makes it easier for people to hear about others getting rich around them. The transition mechanism of spreading the gospel of FOMO is the media. In his book, *Irrational Exuberance,* Nobel Prize winner Robert Shiller says the news media adds fuel to the fire of herd-like thinking in a bubble:

> Although the news media – newspapers, magazines, and broadcast media, along with their new outlets on the Internet – present themselves as detached observers of market events, they are themselves an integral part of their events. Significant market events generally occur only if there is similar thinking among large groups of people, and the news media are essential vehicles for the spread of ideas.[13]

You can't blame the media for every investment thesis that gets blown out of proportion, but it would be difficult to have bubbles if it weren't for the free flow of information. This is why the information age is a double-edged sword. We have access to more information in a day than our ancestors saw in a lifetime, but that fire hose of information can often act as a deterrent to rational thought. The media often fans the flames of groupthink and confirmation bias.

There were just three railway journals at the outset of the 1840s, led by the *Railway Times*. By the time the mania reached its zenith in 1845, there were 14 biweekly railway papers, two daily editions, and one that was published every day in both the morning and the evening. Advertisements flooded the newspapers and periodicals. The media pounced on the Queen Victoria train ride, proclaiming railways as a revolutionary development for mankind, sparking interest from the public in all things rail travel. Hudson was far ahead of the game in terms of understanding the power of the press and how to use it to expand his empire. It helped that he had a financial interest in three newspapers who would all run flattering pieces on his railway projects to attract new investors. There is a rumor that Hudson even tried to support a radical new publication called the *Daily News* and have Charles Dickens as the editor. Dickens was not a fan of Hudson and supposedly remarked, "that he [Dickens] should be the last man in the world to be a supporter of it."[14]

The schemes worked like this: newspaper ads would promise a 10% dividend for anyone who put money into a new railway project. If the project got enough funding, the directors would hold onto a large allocation of shares in the newly formed corporation. This created enough scarcity to push up the price from the flood of new investors, which thereby allowed the directors to flood the market with their shares by selling at a premium price. George Hudson was a master at this scheme, promising unsustainable dividend yields of 50% to inflate the share prices on certain issues, which only encouraged more insider trading by himself and the company directors.[15]

At the start of 1845, 16 new railway proposals were underway and over 50 new companies were formed to meet this demand. Those promoting these deals were highly underestimating the actual costs involved with these projects, often quoting the expenses at bare bones levels for engineering and materials alone, forsaking a staggering amount of ancillary costs. Expenses were purposefully understated to ensure the public would put up the money in the first place and deal with the ramifications and cost overruns later (or not at all once they flipped the shares for a profit). Actual costs turned out to be around twice what was estimated.[16]

In my preparation for this chapter I read a ridiculously long research piece that sought to quantify what was being priced in by the rise in railway stock prices for variables like economic growth, profits, revenues, and the total addressable market of tracks and passengers. No one was doing this at the time. People don't set baseline expectations during a mania. There were plenty of people at the time warning investors how unsustainable these fundamentals were, but no one wants to talk about fundamentals when there's money to be made in the short term.

Because the media was so heavily involved in the mania, the public at large became by far the biggest investors in the bubble. In fact, Parliament published a report in the summer of 1845 revealing the identity of some 20,000 investors who had subscribed for at least £2,000 or more worth of railway stocks. Hudson's name was on there, of course, but so were 157 members of Parliament and almost 260 clergymen.[17] Investors included the likes of Charles Darwin, John Stuart Mill, and the Bronte sisters. Darwin is said to have lost up to 60% in the aftermath of the mania, which was actually much better than most fared in the bloodbath that followed.[18] The rest were mostly regular people, showing how broad the speculation was. Many investors were subscribed for more shares than they could ever hope to pay for, but the idea was they would all have the chance to sell at a premium before getting all of their capital called in to create the actual railway projects. Most people assumed the greater fool theory applied, but no one planned on being the last fool standing. Rarely do investors have the timing or fortitude to turn the greater fool theory into a reality.

The mania was particularly strong in the suburbs because these were the areas that could see the biggest impact from the infrastructure build-out from the new train tracks. In one town, there was a group of stockbrokers who would take an express train twice a day to relay information from one town to the next on the latest changes in share prices for the railway stocks. Practically all the money for construction of the railways came from individuals. By 1850, the amount invested was around £250 million, almost half the GDP of Great Britain at the time, the equivalent of roughly $1.25 trillion for the UK today (or almost $10 trillion for the US in today's terms).[19]

The Other Side

Rising interest rates were the first pinprick in the railway bubble in the summer of 1845. But there were still a record number of Railway Bills in Parliament's 1846 session than ever before or ever since. The appetite for projects remained even after share prices began to dip. There's an old saying that markets take the stairs up but the elevator down, and the railway stocks were no different. Increased competition and overinvestment finally brought these companies back to earth. Bankruptcies hit an all-time high in 1846, just a year after the height of the mania. People from all walks of life and levels of wealth were ruined. By the start of 1850, railway share prices had fallen an astronomical 85% on average.[20]

By 1849, Hudson's role as Railway King came to an unceremonious end. Four of the railway companies he was heavily involved in were under investigation. The shady personal transactions, embezzlement of company funds, overstating of profits, bribing members of Parliament to push his projects through, and insider trading schemes were all made public. The 12 reports produced about his business dealings forever changed public perception of the once revered businessman. The high society Hudson so eagerly sought to be a part of immediately turned their back on him. Hudson was never prosecuted in a court of law because securities laws at the time didn't protect shareholders the way they do now. But he was tried and convicted in the court of public opinion and ostracized by the elite class, which may have been even more of a blow to his gigantic ego.[21]

The press sang Hudson's praises when things were going well but turned their back on him when things went awry. The *Railway Times* published what was basically his business obituary, but they also came down hard on the investors who went along for the ride:

> He no more caused the railway mania than Napoleon caused the French Revolution. He was its child, its ornaments, and its boast. His talent for organisation was prodigious. No labour or speculation seemed too vast for his powers. He combined and systematised the attacks of a hundred bands upon the public purse; he raised all the fares, he lowered the speed, he reduced the establishments, he 'cooked' all the reports, and he trebled all the shares. The shareholders wanted their dividends doubled, and their shares raised to a proportionate market value. They never calculated the extent to which these achievements

were honestly practicable, or considered the measures to which it would be necessary to resort. They wanted the trick done all at once and Hudson was the man to do it.[22]

Hudson was able to stay afloat in political life for a few years after the bubble had burst but was eventually arrested for not paying his debts and died broke a number of years later.

The Silver Lining of a Market Crash

A large number of tech start-ups with seemingly good ideas went out of business after the dot-com flameout. But that era planted the seeds for the next wave of innovation that occurred, which gave us services like YouTube, Facebook, Twitter, and Google. Venture capitalist Marc Andreessen said, "All those ideas are working today. I can't think of a single idea from that era that isn't working today."[23]

The railway boom and bust had some positive outcomes as well. Not all was lost from this period of untamed speculation, greed, and accounting fraud. By 1855, there were over 8,000 miles of railroad track in operation, giving Britain the highest density of railroad tracks in the world, measuring seven times the length of France or Germany. The railways set up during the bubble years came to represent 90% of the total length of the current British railway system. People and businesses across the country experienced massive gains in efficiency through cheaper and faster transportation of raw materials, finished products, and passengers. And during the 1840s more than half a million people were employed by the railway companies to make those tracks a reality. Tens of thousands of people from Ireland were provided employment throughout the famine years. In many ways, this was a wealth transfer from rich and middle-class speculators to the labor class that simultaneously provided the country with much needed transportation infrastructure.[24]

News distribution spread, and the capital markets became more mature. New stock markets were set up in cities all across the country. Stock brokerage firms grew from 6 in 1830 to almost 30 by 1847. There was greater innovation during the industrial revolution of the eighteenth century but the railway boom required far more capital, and thus investors. This changed the way the middle class thought about investing its money.[25]

The problem for those trying to handicap the financial ramifications of this type of innovation is that the economic impact doesn't always occur at the same speed. Investors extrapolate innovation indefinitely into the future, carrying prices too far, too fast. It took time for the combustible engine to completely replace the horse and carriage. The promises of the Internet almost all came true, but we first had to go through the crash and a number of lean years to get there. Excitement pervades when new technologies are released. Most of the early car companies flamed out. When car ownership first took off in the 1920s there were 108 automakers in the US. By the 1950s, they had been whittled down to the big three that produced the majority of cars.[26] The entire airline industry basically lost money or went out of business in the century after air travel was invented.

But investors are so enthusiastic they never stop to wonder what could go wrong, only how the world could change, and more importantly, how rich they could become in the process. The siren song of innovation means there will invariably be a new gold rush every time we collectively get excited about a shiny new object. Those innovations may change the way we live but that doesn't necessarily mean they're going to make you wealthy in the process.

Innovation is one of the many ingredients for fraud to occur. In the next chapter we'll look at how even an outdated product can cause people to collectively lose their minds during a fraud of epic proportions.

Notes

1. Johnson S. *How We Got to Now: Six Innovations That Made the Modern World.* New York: Riverhead Books; 2014.
2. Batnick M. The ghost of tech stocks past. The Irrelevant Investor [Internet] 2018 Jun 30. Available from: https://theirrelevantinvestor. com/2018/06/30/the-ghost-of-tech-stocks-past/
3. McCollough B. An eye-opening look at the dot-com bubble of 2000 – and how it shapes our lives today. Ideas.Ted.com [Internet] 2018 Dec 4. Available from: https://ideas.ted.com/an-eye-opening-look-at-the-dot-com-bubble-of-2000-and-how-it-shapes-our-lives-today/
4. Railway Mania. Winton [Internet]. 2018 Sep 18. Available from: https://www.winton.com/longer-view/railway-mania
5. Chancellor E. *Devil Take the Hindmost: A History of Financial Speculation.* New York: Plume; 2000.
6. Arnold AJ and McCartney S. George Hudson: *The Rise and Fall of the Railway King.* London: Hambledon Continuum; 2004.
7. Railway Mania. Winton [Internet]. 2018 Sep 18. Available from: https://www.winton.com/longer-view/railway-mania

8. Arnold AJ and McCartney S. George Hudson: *The Rise and Fall of the Railway King*. London: Hambledon Continuum; 2004.
9. Chancellor E. *Devil Take the Hindmost: A History of Financial Speculation*. New York: Plume; 2000.
10. Arnold AJ and McCartney S. George Hudson: the rise and fall of the railway king. London: Hambledon Continuum; 2004.
11. Chancellor E. *Devil Take the Hindmost: A History of Financial Speculation*. New York: Plume; 2000.
12. Arnold AJ and McCartney S. George Hudson: *The Rise and Fall of the Railway King*. London: Hambledon Continuum; 2004.
13. Shiller RJ. Irrational exuberance. Princeton, New Jersey: Princeton University Press; 2000.
14. Chancellor E. *Devil Take the Hindmost: A History of Financial Speculation*. New York: Plume; 2000.
15. Railway Mania. Winton [Internet]. 2018 Sep 18. Available from: https://www.winton.com/longer-view/railway-mania
16. Odlyzko A. Collective hallucinations and inefficient markets: the British railway mania of the 1840s. SSRN. 2010 Jan 15. doi: https://dx.doi.org/10.2139/ssrn.1537338
17. Chancellor E. *Devil Take the Hindmost: A History of Financial Speculation*. New York: Plume; 2000.
18. Odlyzko A. Collective hallucinations and inefficient markets: the British railway mania of the 1840s. SSRN. 2010 Jan 15. doi: https://dx.doi.org/10.2139/ssrn.1537338
19. Ibid.
20. Chancellor E. *Devil Take the Hindmost: A History of Financial Speculation*. New York: Plume; 2000.
21. Arnold AJ and McCartney S. George Hudson: *The Rise and Fall of the Railway King*. London: Hambledon Continuum; 2004.
22. The Railway Times. 1849 Apr 10. pg. 5.
23. Ritholtz B. Transcript: Andreessen MIB podcast. The Big Picture [Internet]. 2017 May 28. Available from: https://ritholtz.com/2017/05/transcript-andreessen-mib-podcast/
24. Chancellor, E. *Devil Take the Hindmost: A History of Financial Speculation*. New York: Plume; 2000.
25. Arnold AJ and McCartney S. George Hudson: *The Rise and Fall of the Railway King*. London: Hambledon Continuum; 2004.
26. Irwin N. It's a winner-take-all world, whether you like it or note. *The Atlantic* [Internet]. 2019 Jun 17. Available from: https://www.theatlantic.com/ideas/archive/2019/06/its-a-winner-take-all-world-heres-how-to-get-ahead/591700/

CHAPTER 9

The Seductive Power of FOMO

Everything in life is founded on confidence.

—Ivar Kreuger

Thomas Edison invented the first electric light bulb in 1879. This innovation changed the world in immense ways but it didn't happen overnight. Not a single home was wired for electricity over the year following Edison's breakthrough, but by 1940 nearly 100% of urban homes were wired.[1] In the intervening years, people still had to do something for light and warmth. It's hard to imagine now what with the ubiquity of electricity, but matches were a consumer staple in the late-nineteenth and early-twentieth century. They didn't fall too far behind food, clothing, and a roof over your head in the pecking order of household necessities. Matches were used in a variety of ways – to light kerosene lamps, gas heaters, candles, fires, stoves, and everyone's favorite deadly habit back then – smoking. Cigarette production in the US doubled in the decade ending in 1929, so matches were used for both needs and vices.

The Swedes were the first to develop the safe phosphorous surface used to light a match by striking it against the side of a matchbox. They were called safety matches at the time and became an enormous hit. This innovation quickly turned Sweden into the

97

biggest exporter of matches in the world. By the 1920s, one Swedish man controlled three-quarters of the production and sales of all matches used in the world, owning more than 200 match factories in 35 different countries all around the globe.[2]

Many frauds start from a legitimate business or idea that gets taken too far from some combination of greed, loose morals, and overconfidence. Once the ball gets rolling, money begins pouring in, and a certain amount of power is obtained, it becomes difficult to turn off the spigot. Certain people will do just about anything to ensure money and power continue indefinitely. And so it was with the Match King from Sweden, Ivar Kreuger.

On October 28, 1929, Kreuger appeared on the cover of *Time* magazine. He was the most talked about person in the United States at the time because he was rich, powerful, and mysterious. The Match King owned a private island in the North Sea and apartments all over the world. Greta Garbo, a fellow Swede and famous actress, was his good friend.[3] President Herbert Hoover asked for his advice in business matters during private meetings. Kreuger played a prominent role in the Nobel Prize ceremonies and had business dealings with world leaders and prime ministers. Elon Musk is a decent modern-day comparison in terms of celebrity, but Kreuger was more mysterious. There were even plans to use his story to depict the American dream in a full feature-length film. That film never saw the light of day because he shot and killed himself shortly thereafter in 1932 as his empire of fraud crumbled all around him.[4]

How to Create a Monopoly

To understand how Kreuger got into this position in the first place we have to go back to the beginning of his business dealings. The man started out as an engineer, and even worked in the US for some time, but by 1907 returned to Stockholm where, with Paul Toll, he formed the construction firm of Kreuger & Toll. A few years later he would enter the match business, using Kreuger & Toll as something of a holding company for his other investments and match factory purchases.[5]

International Match Corporation quickly became one of the largest players in the match industry worldwide, mainly because of the CEO's take-no-prisoners approach to business. The first step in the process involved entering a local market and selling at local prices with a higher-quality product to grab market share. Once International Match owned the market and later the local factory, they would lower the quality of the matches to save money. Match factories were modernized, and sales would be expanded overseas. Kreuger also purchased the companies that made the machines for production to reduce costs and increase efficiency in the factories. The enigmatic CEO was far ahead of his peers, going so far as to predict in advance how the United Kingdom abandoning the gold standard would open up international finance and trade. Kreuger wanted in on a more globalized economy but more importantly, he wanted the ability to raise prices by cornering the market and creating a monopoly. By 1915, he controlled ten match factories in Sweden alone. Kreuger's growing collection of companies began making money by year two and was one of the few profitable European companies during World War I, a period that decimated businesses around the globe. But the match business was highly competitive and had few barriers to entry. Competition was driving down prices. He knew he needed monopoly power to make it last.[6]

Kreuger's business plan boiled down to a loan-for-monopoly trade. To gain access to match companies in different countries, one of Kreuger's companies would loan money to needy countries at favorable terms so that government officials from those countries would then allow him to buy up the local match factories. It was an I'll-scratch-your-back-if-you-scratch-mine business strategy. This gave International Match free reign in countries such as Poland, Peru, Greece, Ecuador, Hungary, Estonia, Yugoslavia, Romania, and Latvia. The *Time* magazine cover story explained it like this:

> From the standpoint of a government that is not too proud to monopolize, business done with Herr Kreuger is good business. The government gets large sums of needed cash and then repays the loan by a tax on matches.[7]

These loans were typically paying him back 6–8% interest while his match company and financial holding company regularly paid out double-digit dividends to investors, up to 25–30% at their peak. It doesn't take a genius to understand that receiving 6–8% while simultaneously paying out 20–30% isn't a winning trade. There would need to be massive profits to make up for this inherent shortfall in the interest rate spread. Because of the times, no investor even bothered to ask how this was possible.

No one bothered to ask about the underlying financials of Kreuger's companies either. And if they did ask, they didn't get truthful answers. No one else besides Kreuger knew what the actual profit and loss numbers looked like for International Match or his holding company. Kreuger deceived investors, board members, and auditors alike by forming around 400 different off-the-book conduits to move money around and hide what was really going on. No one had a clue how these loan deals worked or what the terms were. At one point he told the board of directors for International Match that Spain would be paying 16% interest on a loan he extended the country. The only other person who saw the loan documents thought they were fake. Kreuger lived by the Napoleon saying, "one first-class brain is enough for an army."[8] This line of thinking would come back to haunt him.

When board members would visit his office, Kreuger used a dummy phone where he would pretend to have conversations with world leaders. "Good morning, Prime Minister!" he would exclaim to a dead phone line. Percy Rockefeller, the nephew of John D. Rockefeller, was a member of the board of directors. At one point he was so impressed with these fake phone calls that he told the other directors, "He [Kreuger] is on the most intimate terms with the heads of European Governments. Gentlemen, we are fortunate indeed to be associated with Ivar Kreuger."

One of the defining characteristics of someone who takes advantage of others financially is the ability to make people believe what you're saying. Kreuger knew how to read a room and get people to believe in him because he acted as if he knew exactly what he was doing. Even President Herbert Hoover leaned heavily on Kreuger during the 1929 crash for advice on how to proceed during the onset of the Great Depression.[9] The guy who was running one of the biggest financial frauds in history was being relied upon to offer business advice to the president of the United States. This would have been like Barack Obama asking Bernie Madoff how to handle the Great Financial Crisis.

The Roaring 20s

When technology moves forward by leaps and bounds, as it did in the first part of the twentieth century, people prefer betting on the future more than betting on the past. For Kreuger, the past was selling matches while the future was selling financial securities. No one really knows why but something shifted in his business strategy around 1923 or 1924. A good guess would be an insatiable desire for money and power with an environment that was ripe for those looking for both. Up until that point it appears he was running a legitimate business enterprise.

The 1920s were a breeding ground for financial fraud and malfeasance. Kreuger went from businessman to stock promoter, industrialist to financier, and, by all accounts, a moderately honest man to an outright fraud. His match business made little progress in the 1920s, but the holding companies he created sold a variety of securities worth $250 million in the United States alone (that's around $3.6 billion in today's dollars). The *Wall Street Journal* sang his praises for the innovative ways he was raising capital. One securities analyst said of his 1923 IPO, "it was like touching a match to a bucket of gasoline." None of the companies actually had any assets. Investors went nuts in the 1920s for anything to do with Wall Street. Money was being made hand over fist, and the fear of missing out was maybe as strong as it's ever been, before or since. The number of Americans who paid taxes on at least $1 million of income a year or more quadrupled by the end of the 1920s. Newly issued financial securities jumped from 690 in 1923 to almost 2,000 by 1929. Bank loans to investors grew fourfold in this time.[10]

Investors were in the market for "too good to be true" in the 1920s and that's exactly what the Match King gave them. From 1923 to 1929, Kreuger tripled his funds raised in America. Many of the deals involved complex derivative products. Investors placed such a premium on the securities he was putting up for sale that he began making more money from the appreciation of these securities than the actual loans they were set up to finance.

Forming a new company was as simple as filling out a piece of paper at that time so Kreuger would set up a new holding company and transfer money from one of his existing companies to the new one. Voila! A new company with no true assets but good enough to fool unwitting investors. To paraphrase Dickens, fraud becomes much easier to commit when it was the best of times and when it was the worst of times. The 1920s were the best of times, but they morphed into the worst of times.

Kreuger wanted to prove he belonged with the elites of the world and what better proving ground than the greatest wealth machine on the planet. I think he truly believed all of his lies and fraudulent activities would reverse some day if he could only hold things together for a little longer. And he almost did it too, if it wasn't for the greatest stock market crash the world had ever seen.

When the Tide Goes Out

Kreuger once claimed, "There is not a single competitor with sufficient influence upon the different markets to cause us any really serious harm. No market is sufficiently significant to be of importance to us."[11] That may have been true in the match business but there was another market he should have been even more concerned with – the stock market.

Warren Buffett once said, "Only when the tide goes out do you discover who's been swimming naked." The tide had never gone out as much as it did during the Great Depression, and it revealed there was a massive number of people who forgot to wear their swim trunks in the lead-up to this massive market crash and economic downturn. By early 1929, investments in his financial holding company, Kreuger & Toll, were the most widely distributed securities in the world. They were selling at an unbelievable 730% premium to par value (or their intrinsic worth). Then the floor fell out from underneath the market, as stocks cratered in the fall of 1929. On October 24, 1929, the Dow Jones Industrial Average fell 11%. Four days later the Dow fell another 13%. The roaring 20s came to a screeching halt without warning.

Time magazine almost immediately regretted their decision to put Kreuger on their cover because the market crashed the very same week. They quickly changed their tune by following it up with another story that offered doubts about his scheme and the company's ability to continue to pay such lofty dividends. Investors didn't seem to care just yet. During 1929 Kreuger worried investors would abandon ship so he raised the dividend from 25% to 30% and prayed the downturn would end in short order. It didn't. From June 1931 until December of that same year, his securities fell in value as much as 80% right along with the stock market.

A defining characteristic of charlatans is the ability to immediately move the goalposts and try to shift the blame when things go wrong. Kreuger wanted nothing to do with taking responsibility for his actions. Instead of accepting blame for overleveraging his companies, Kreuger complained his businesses, "have been the subject of a deceitful press campaign from…some twenty blackmailing papers who continually attack our securities." He began spouting off conspiracy theories about an internationally organized short-selling syndicate that was out to get him.[12]

Kreuger's businesses all took a dive during the Great Depression, but it took a few years for his house of cards to completely fall apart. Not only was business slowing, but he had margined up the securities for his businesses, several times in many cases, faking the collateral on the issues. By 1932, Kreuger had 225 subsidiaries, including one in every developed country outside of Russia. He created monopolies in 24 countries and loaned out almost as $400 million to European governments at a time when many of them were struggling to borrow money. These loans actually helped some of these countries rebuild their infrastructure and stabilize their exchange rates following the first World War.

Not only did he control the largest match company in the world, he also owned real estate, telephone companies, newspapers, mining companies, and banks. But this mighty empire couldn't withstand the brutal financial markets of the Great Depression. Kreuger shot and killed himself on March 12, 1932. An audit after the fact revealed his companies were bankrupt. Claims against his estate were more than $1 billion. When he took his own life, few people realized the size and scale of the fraud Kreuger had pulled off. This was one of the most well-known, wealthiest, respected businessmen in the world. Why would he do such a thing?[13]

Not a Ponzi but Close Enough

Kreuger wasn't running a Ponzi scheme in the traditional sense. If anything, the scale of his operation was much larger and lasted much longer than what Charles Ponzi tried to pull off. Plus, Kreuger raised 50 times as much money and lasted 10 times as long as Ponzi. At certain points, he was paying off old investors with newly raised money but even he knew that couldn't last forever. In many ways, he was running legitimate businesses. The problem is he wasn't allocating capital very well and he made promises he couldn't possibly hope to keep because the company and its securities were so heavily indebted. High dividend payouts helped avoid too many questions, but it also made it nearly impossible to work over the long term as a viable business model. It was simply a matter of continuously raising outside capital to keep up the façade.

The Match King also had complete control over the funds produced by his collection of businesses and he did what he pleased with those funds. Kreuger kept the books for his vast enterprise but he chose not to share that information with investors or even his employees. The books were fudged in both good and bad years to balance things out. His belief was he just needed business to grow enough to be able to continue paying high dividends to pay off their earlier debts. But when your burn rate exceeds your revenue by a factor of almost five-to-one, eventually you're going to go broke. There was never an explanation on the financial statements about how this conglomerate made so much money. The largest category was "Profits from other investments." To keep the auditors at bay he would simply tell them his deals with governments were politically sensitive and couldn't be disclosed.[14]

Following his death, auditors claimed the companies were completely insolvent. Balance sheets grossly misrepresented the financial standing and assets in the company. The losses were more than the national debt of Sweden. The accountants who combed through the books proclaimed the balance sheets of his holding company, Kreuger & Toll, "grossly misrepresent the true financial position of the company," and the fraudulent entries were made "under the personal direction of the late Mr. Kreuger." Congressional debates called him "the greatest swindler in all history." A year later Congress created the SEC and gave Americans the right to sue companies for fraud. Some claimed his company's collapse was "probably the strongest activating force..." for creating those new provisions and regulations.[15]

The Seductive Power of FOMO

The brain of someone high on cocaine or morphine expecting to get another fix is indistinguishable from someone looking to make money on their investments.[16] This applies not only to investors looking to score a quick return on their capital but also to those con artists who orchestrated these frauds. There are small gateway drugs in the business of fraud as well. This is one of the main reasons we humans almost always take things too far in the markets. We become addicted to gains, and once those gains are achieved it takes a bigger hit each time to satisfy our needs. The fear of missing out, or FOMO, results from watching others get rich, which typically provides the lighter fluid on the fire that is a raging bull market. Keeping with this same analogy, investors were basically using dynamite to fan the flames in the 1920s.

All these years later, there still isn't a great explanation for what triggered the Great Depression. Fred Schwed shared an anecdote in his book, *Where Are the Customers' Yachts*, that comes close to describing why it occurred:

> In 1929, there was a luxurious club car which ran each weekday morning into Pennsylvania Station. Near the door there was placed a silver bowl with a quantity of nickels in it. Those who needed a nickel in change for the subway ride downtown took one. They were not expected to put anything back in exchange; this was not money – it was one of those minor inconveniences like a quill toothpick for which nothing is charged. It was only five cents.
> There have been many explanations of the sudden debacle of October, 1929. The explanation I prefer is that the eye of Jehovah, a wrathful god, happened to chance in October upon that bowl. In sudden understandable annoyance, Jehovah kicked over the financial structure of the United States, and thus saw to it that the bowl of free nickels disappeared forever.[17]

Kreuger had been collecting from that bowl for most of the decade, except his scheme involved a lot more than nickels. The Match King's financial scam had just the right mix of money, power, influence, obedience, secrecy, and the promise of massive profits all coming together during an absolute powder keg of a market environment. And it's not like Kreuger's investors were the only ones making money during that time. Everyone in the markets was getting rich. People almost felt entitled to profits in the roaring 20s. Why should everyone else get rich but not me?

Kreuger's fraud checked all the boxes for the perfect storm to commit a massive fraud. The 1920s were a time of great technological change and innovation. The list of inventions that were rolled out during this decade is staggering. There was the automobile, the washing machine, the airplane, the radio, the refrigerator, the instant camera, the electric razor, the jukebox, the garbage disposal, and the television, to name a few. When people experience such rapid change in their lives you almost can't blame them for getting greedy and extrapolating the current pace of innovation and growth into the foreseeable future.

The infrastructure of modern financial markets was still under construction so innovations in financial securities further enticed people to take unnecessary risks with their money. The tracks for the future were being laid in front of people's eyes. Markets were booming but Kreuger was also promising massive financial returns to his investors. People wanted to believe, so no one questioned his actions because it seemed like he had his hand on the steering wheel the entire time. When things are going swimmingly, no one bothers to ask questions about complexity or financial statement trickery.

One of the hardest things to do as an investor is to keep your wits about you when everyone else is going mad. This is especially true when there's an enigmatic figurehead overseeing the operation. A well-known British writer at the time called Kreuger, "The best-liked crook that ever lived." One of his closest colleagues said, "There was an odd air of greatness about Ivar. I think he could get people to do anything. They fell for him, they couldn't resist his peculiar charm and magnetism."[18]

Leverage and ego mixed with a bull market can be a lethal combination. Sprinkle in a massive fraud and you've got a nasty cocktail that can only lead to poor outcomes for all involved.

Notes

1. *Gordon R J. The Rise and Fall of American Growth: The U.S. Standard of Living Since the Civil War.* Princeton, New Jersey: Princeton University Press; 2016.
2. Train J. *Famous Financial Fiascos.* New York: Random House; 1984.
3. Monopolist. *Time: The Weekly Magazine* [Internet]. 1929 Oct 28. Available from: http://content.time.com/time/covers/0,16641,19291028,00.html
4. Partnoy F. *The Match King: Ivar Kreuger, The Financial Genius Behind a Century of Wall Street Scandals.* New York: Public Affairs; 2009.
5. Monopolist. *Time: The Weekly Magazine* [Internet]. 1929 Oct 28. Available from: http://content.time.com/time/covers/0,16641,19291028,00.html
6. Partnoy F. *The Match King: Ivar Kreuger, The Financial Genius Behind a Century of Wall Street Scandals.* New York: Public Affairs; 2009.
7. Monopolist. *Time: The Weekly Magazine* [Internet]. 1929 Oct 28. Available from: http://content.time.com/time/covers/0,16641,19291028,00.html
8. Train J. *Famous Financial Fiascos.* New York: Random House; 1984.
9. Ibid.
10. Partnoy F. *The Match King: Ivar Kreuger, The Financial Genius Behind a Century of Wall Street Scandals.* New York: Public Affairs; 2009.

11. Monopolist. *Time: The Weekly Magazine* [Internet]. 1929 Oct 28. Available from: http://content.time.com/time/covers/0,16641,19291028,00.html
12. Partnoy F. *The Match King: Ivar Kreuger, The Financial Genius Behind a Century of Wall Street Scandals.* New York: Public Affairs; 2009.
13. MacLeish A. A 3-part series on the life and death of Ivar Kreuger. *Fortune* [Internet]. 1933 May 1. Available from: http://fortune.com/1933/05/01/a-3-part-series-on-the-life-and-death-of-ivar-kreuger/
14. Partnoy F. *The Match King: Ivar Kreuger, The Financial Genius Behind a Century of Wall Street Scandals.* New York: Public Affairs; 2009.
15. MacLeish A. A 3-part series on the life and death of Ivar Kreuger. *Fortune* [Internet]. 1933 May 1. Available from: http://fortune.com/1933/05/01/a-3-part-series-on-the-life-and-death-of-ivar-kreuger/
16. Zweig J. *Your Money and Your Brain: How the New Science of Neuroeconomics Can Make You Rich.* New York: Simon & Schuster; 2007.
17. Schwed F. Where are the customers' yachts? or a good hard look at Wall Street. Hoboken, New Jersey: John Wiley & Sons; 2006.
18. Partnoy F. *The Match King: Ivar Kreuger, The Financial Genius Behind a Century of Wall Street Scandals.* New York: Public Affairs; 2009.

CHAPTER

10

Type I Charlatan

Anyone can create money; the problem lies in getting it accepted.
—Hyman Minsky

From 1853 through 1933, the United States experienced a recession or depression once every 3.9 years. The average contraction in GDP during this time was a ghastly 23%. Each of those 22 economic downturns, save for one, saw GDP fall by double digits (and the remaining instance saw GDP fall 9.7%.)

Contrast these numbers with the period from 1934 through 2018. The last time there was a double-digit contraction in GDP was in the short recession of 1945 following World War II. Before that it was the 1937–1938 downturn. The Great Recession of 2007–2009 saw GDP fall a little over 5%, a blip on the radar screen compared to the late-nineteenth and early-twentieth century economic experience. Since 1933, the average recession in the US has seen economic growth fall by an average of just 4.3%. The two longest economic expansions in US history have both come since 1990.

There are several explanations you could offer as to why recessions have gotten shallower over time while expansions have lasted longer. The US was basically an emerging market back then. We have a far more mature, diverse, and dynamic economy now. But the reason I chose 1933 as the cut-off point, aside from the fact it was towards the end of the Great Depression, is that was the year Franklin D. Roosevelt took the US off the gold standard. An act of Congress severed the tie between gold and the dollar, effectively allowing the price of gold to float more freely and giving the Federal Reserve more ammunition to fight the forces of inflation and deflation without being hamstrung by having our currency backed by a yellow rock.

Central banks and paper currencies are by no means perfect, and they don't prevent developed nations such as the US from experiencing recessions. But it would be foolish to think they haven't played a role in making our economy more stable over time. The Fed acts as something of a lender of last resort for the banking system, which is one of the reasons we didn't have a run on the banks in 2008 and fall into a deep depression. Central banks also set short-term interest rates and manage the flow of credit when necessary, which acts as a shock absorber to the system.

Not everyone agrees with the modern monetary system we have in place, but it's much better than the alternative of massive inflationary booms and deflationary busts every few years in the old system. In fact, the US didn't have a true central bank until 1913. There were attempts to create such a structure on numerous occasions, but the banking system remained disorganized, inefficient, and antiquated until the panic of 1907 forced government officials to make a change. That was the year John Pierpont Morgan single-handedly saved the banking system from complete collapse by lending his own money and basically forcing other banks to do the same to keep the system afloat. A banker sent Morgan a note at the time that read, "the safety and welfare of the financial structure of this country depends almost entirely upon you." The Federal Reserve Act of 1913 was created in the aftermath of this panic which set in place the current monetary system used today.[1]

The seeds for today's paper money system predate the creation of the Fed. In the early-eighteenth century, a Scotsman named John Law was basically the Christopher Columbus of the modern monetary system. Law was just so far ahead of his time that his ideas created a mania that morphed into a scheme that defrauded people out of their life savings in the Mississippi bubble.

John Law and the Mississippi Company

It's easy to spend money in the modern world through the swipe of a card, the click of a button on your phone or computer, or even, God forbid, paying with cold hard cash. But back in the early-eighteenth century, all forms of currency were hard to carry, store, use, or save because there wasn't a single currency in circulation. There was no paper money in most countries either. Gold and other precious metals acted as the currency of the day.

John Law spent a number of years studying the monetary system as a young man, always in search of ways to make the financial system efficient. People were sick of carrying around sacks of gold or silver coins everywhere to buy stuff. Not only did Law want to create a paper monetary system, a novel concept at the time, but he also wanted more money in circulation to give governments more control over the supply of money that wasn't tied to a set amount of gold or silver stored in a vault somewhere. Law wanted to create more inflation to increase prosperity. Banks could always increase the money supply by making loans to citizens and businesses, but Law's breakthrough idea was that credit should reflect the strength or weakness of a country's economy, not how much gold it possessed. The only problem was finding a country willing to give these ideas a shot in the real world.[2]

Enter France, where King Louis XIV had an insatiable need to spend money. The country was on the verge of financial ruin through a combination of excessive debt levels from multiple wars and a corrupt monarch who spent far too lavishly. The nation was willing to get creative to pay off its debts, as many in the government were worried about a revolution from its citizens.[3] Government debt was still a relatively new phenomenon in the late-seventeenth and early-eighteenth centuries, and as with most new shiny new toys they didn't know how to use it responsibly.

When he died after 72 years on the throne, Louis XIV left the heir to his throne, his five-year-old son Louis XV, not a huge pile of money but a huge pile of debt. The boy's uncle Philippe became Regent to oversee the country's finances until the young King came of age. The debt was so severe there was talk of national bankruptcy.[4] Law buddied up to the Regent, informing him that France's debt woes could be solved using a new monetary system. What did they have to lose? How many politicians in their right mind would turn down such a proposition?

Law's proposed monetary system had a number of moving parts. Step one was to create a paper currency that people would receive by turning in their gold and silver. Step two was to run a central bank that controlled the supply of that paper currency to increase or decrease the supply of credit used in the economy. So far this sounds eerily similar to the current system, established after we did away with the gold standard. Step three is where Law's plan would go off the rails. People weren't quite ready to put their full faith behind a paper currency that wasn't backed by anything beyond trust in the system, so Law's regrettable decision at the time was to back paper money with government debt that could then be converted into shares of the Mississippi Company.

France controlled a large part of the United States at that point, so the Mississippi Company was established to take advantage of its resources. It was a development company that received a 25-year lease on France's Louisiana Territory, which gave them a monopoly on discoveries and trade routes.[5] The company hoped to strike it rich by finding gold. Shares were offered to the public but there was a twist. Not only would investors receive shares in the company, much like someone today would buy stock in Apple, Amazon, or Google, but they would do so by exchanging their holdings in government debt or annuities for shares in the company. In effect, this was a debt-for-equity swap.

Imagine loaning money to a friend to be paid back with interest to help them buy a house. But then that friend offers you shares in their newly formed treasure expedition company in exchange for the loan you gave them. Your friend's debts to you would be cleared and you would get any upside if treasure was discovered. But if you were given a faulty map and no treasure was ever discovered…

France assumed it would find more than enough precious metals in the Louisiana Territory to make up for Law's newly issued paper currency. The government basically signed on for this plan immediately because it would relieve their enormous war debts. And investors signed on because the company was paying generous dividends and they had Law, a growing celebrity presence due to his perceived intelligence on economic matters. All classes of French people ate up this idea, as investors were regaled with tales of gold, boundless opportunities, and fabulous riches. This opened the floodgates for the transfer of government debt into shares of the Mississippi Company, which was a huge departure from the sound monetary banking principles Law had learned and preached to others.[6]

With a new financial system in place, liquidity for investors, and the desire to get rich quickly, the value of the company skyrocketed. No one bothered to look into the Mississippi Company's business plan or the risk involved in swapping government debt for shares in this newly formed, unproven venture. Rising prices attract buyers just as falling prices attract sellers so as the price doubled in short order, more investors flocked to trade in their government debt for shares. Stocks are sexy when they're rising while boring old bonds are never going to feel sexy to own.

Law became an instant celebrity. Although he was not Catholic at the time, people assumed the man had divine powers. In 1720, John Dalrymple wrote, "There can be no doubt of John Law's catholicity since he has proved transubstantiation by changing paper into money."[7] Law may have understood monetary policy but he vastly underestimated the toxic mix his policies could create when combined with human nature.

Berkshire Hathaway vice chairman Charlie Munger once asked, "How could economics not be behavioral? If it isn't behavioral, what the hell is it?" Law failed to account for the emotions – greed, envy, overconfidence, hope, and fear – money can bring out in people.

Speculation Is a Hell of a Drug

Rick James famously said on *The Chappelle Show*, "Cocaine is a hell of a drug," when trying to explain his more outlandish behavior during the height of his popularity as a pop singer in the 1980s. For Law, you could substitute the word success for cocaine and the same would be true of many of his decisions once the Mississippi mania got out of hand. Success can intoxicate and corrupt even the brightest of minds.

The highest of nobility in France sought the company of Law and his family. With his newfound wealth, he purchased lavish estates in different parts of the country. Writers and poets were constantly showering him with adulation in their scribes. Law required troops on horseback to escort him wherever he went for a time to clear the streets from onlookers who wanted to meet the man of the hour. Law could do no wrong in the eyes of the public or the government.[8]

For investors in the Mississippi Company, speculation was also a hell of a drug. This mania didn't discriminate by class or wealth.

Both the upper and lower classes were overcome with greed as visions of dollar signs danced in their heads. These are just some of the many crazy stats and stories courtesy of this bubble:

- The share price quadrupled between August and December of 1719 as the country assumed it had figured out the path to easy riches.[9]
- In August 1719, the Mississippi Company took over the entire national debt of France.[10]
- At its height, the market capitalization of the Mississippi Company exceeded the entire GDP of France.[11]
- Cobblers figured out they could make more money renting out their benches for people waiting to buy shares than making shoes.[12]
- It's estimated more than 300,000 people from all over the world came into the country looking to get rich. Living space became such a problem with so many people flocking to the area that houses renting for $200/year skyrocketed to $4,000/month.[13]
- Speculation ran so rampant this was one of the first times in history the word "millionaire" entered the vernacular to describe the new fortunes being created.[14]
- Houses that would typically lease for an annual rent of 1,000 livres were going for 12 to 16 times that amount.
- There's a famous tale that a hunchbacked man earned a decent chunk of change simply by acting as a writing surface to speculators filling out paperwork on the busy streets.[15]

Then there's the story of a doctor who was feeling a patient's pulse. He shrieked, "It falls! It falls! Good God! It falls, it continually falls!" So the woman cried out, "I'm dying! It falls! It falls!" The doctor became puzzled, asking, "What falls?" To which the woman replied, "My pulse! I must be dying!" The doctor then explained he was simply yelling about the price of his shares owned in the Mississippi Company, which were dropping like a brick.[16]

The bubble may have come from intellectual monetary underpinnings, but it was a bubble nonetheless and it was beginning to take on a life of its own. Like most economists, Law created policies based on theories that would work well in a vacuum, minus the element of human nature. Unfortunately, the human element is often the overriding variable in economic outcomes. The use of borrowed money to buy shares in the Mississippi Company was simultaneously propping up the share price and making the system more vulnerable as stock was being purchased on margin.

The share price of the company increased seemingly every day for a time, which only led Law to create more shares in the company, a virtuous cycle. This probably seemed like a great idea at the time, kind of like how a fourth beer always seems like a good idea after you've already had three. At this stage in the game, the government could have offered the drunks (speculators) a million beers (shares) and they would've accepted them. The Regent who initially backed Law knew next to nothing about finance but assumed the fact that things were going well in the present meant things would continue to go well into the future. Keeping with our drinking analogy, these people wanted to spend all night getting wasted without ever having to deal with the hangover in the morning. The other problem is Law was spiking people's cocktails by giving the drunks borrowed money to buy more shares.

The financial markets are a cruel mistress who always follows up a raging night out with a wicked hangover in the morning. The problem is no one knows how late those parties will last. Sometimes they end at midnight. Other times, to quote Calvin Broadus (aka Snoop Dogg), "they ain't leavin' till six in the mornin'." The Mississippi bubble went the distance in its frenzy of speculation. Law convinced the Regent if some paper currency exchanged for government debt was good, then more had to be better. The higher the share price, the more shares of Mississippi Company stock he issued to take advantage.[17]

Pop Goes the Bubble

The supply of shares eventually overwhelmed the demand, and prices finally took a breather. This is when Law panicked. As prices fell, he instructed the central bank to buy shares, but that could only last for so long as they eventually reached a breaking point. He also tried guaranteeing investors that the new shares offered would trade at par value within six months, which would be a doubling of their money. This was a gamble that didn't work.[18]

The currency initially traded at a premium to its intrinsic stated value which caused something Law did not anticipate – people began selling their shares to buy more tangible assets. Using his sway with government officials, Law tried to enact rules and regulations which would stem the tide and make the precious metals like gold and silver harder to utilize as currencies, but the damage had already been done.[19]

Prices fell 90% as shares eventually became worthless because the remaining value was well under the amount people borrowed to purchase them. Law had to be protected by guards. He fled to Holland as his life was in danger from the angry mob. Citizens went from being millionaires to being broke within a week's time. Law himself stated, "Last year I was the richest individual who ever lived. Today I have nothing, not even enough to keep alive."[20] It's important to remember that an economy that utilizes paper currency is based on faith more than anything. The people of France not only invested their money in Law's system, but also their trust. Once that faith was broken and investor confidence was shattered it was lights out.

The biggest problem with the Mississippi Company was that it never actually made any money in the trade business. In fact, the company never really even tried. Unfortunately, no one bothered to even look into the matter because everyone was so worried about making money. That included John Law. Not a single ship from the Mississippi Company ever even departed for the shores of Louisiana. The business itself was basically an afterthought in this mania. Law died broke, nine years after the height of the bubble, in Venice.

The public lost faith in the French banking system, and the country found it challenging to borrow money for years to come. Law's ideas were so ahead of their time, and his response to the bubble was so badly played, his scheme likely set the French economy back decades because its citizens and government officials basically revolted against the stock market from this experience. It was a disaster of epic proportions. Voltaire observed, "Paper money has now been restored to its intrinsic value." It took decades for France's monetary system to recover. Law's debacle inadvertently led to the start of the French Revolution in 1789 as this was the first chink in the armor of the French monarchy. France didn't go back to the use of paper currency until 1793, and people were so scared of what it could do they were forced to use it through the threat of the guillotine.[21]

Type I and Type II Charlatans

When testing a hypothesis using statistics, there are two types of errors a statistician can make. A type I error is when you reject a null hypothesis that is actually true. A type II error is when you accept a null hypothesis that is actually false. These terms are a bit technical, so allow me to explain using a meme. The best example floating around the Internet is a picture of a man on the left and a picture of a pregnant woman on the right. The picture of the man on the left shows a doctor telling him he is pregnant. This is a type I error or a false positive. The picture of the pregnant woman on the right shows the doctor telling her she is not pregnant. This is a type II error, or a false negative.

You can think about charlatans who take people for all they're worth much in the same way. There are two types of charlatans in the world. Type I charlatans are the visionaries who are more or less sincere but wind up ruining their investors anyways because they take their ideas to the extreme or fail to account for the unintended consequences. These false positive charlatans are so passionate that it becomes difficult for the victims of fraud to see any downside. When you combine intellect, passion, and people who would like to make a boatload of money, it's easy to develop blind spots to potential risks involved in these schemes. And once a Type I charlatan gets a taste of success, it's tough to pull in the reins when things go wrong. No one wants to admit their life's work turned out to be a fraud.

Type II charlatans are the out-and-out fraudsters who blatantly set out to take people for all they're worth. These hucksters are only interested in making as much money as possible and they don't care who gets hurt to achieve that goal. These are the false-negative charlatans because their marks assume these hucksters are acting in their best interest but in reality they're nothing but frauds. It's difficult for victims of fraud to see through this type of charlatan because they know exactly how to sell you. They understand the patterns of human behavior and tell you exactly what you want to hear. They move the goalposts and shift the blame when it appears they're wrong and understand how to massage your ego to keep you in line. Schemes from Type II charlatans are difficult to avoid because there are always those who can be charmed by a good sales pitch from an intelligent-sounding fraud.

Both Type I and Type II charlatans allow their ambitions to take over, especially during a financial mania. It appears as if they can do no wrong so they start to believe the hype. John Law is a classic case of a Type I charlatan. The man was far ahead of his time when it came to ideas about the monetary system, but he was a charlatan nonetheless. Law never had a doubt his project would work. He assumed France would come out of this affair as the richest, most powerful nation in the world. Law invested his money back into the country, a truly believer it was going to work. It's not like he was pocketing money and investing it in other countries. He kept it all in France with the understanding that his ideas were gold.[22]

There is still debate today whether Law was brilliant or a complete fraud. I think there's room for both sides to be true. Law was an intelligent fraud, a genius who didn't understand the downside of his own theories and completely underestimated the toxic mix leverage and quick riches can have on the herd mentality. You can be both a genius and a charlatan. The two are not mutually exclusive.

When Law met with the nobility of France in something of an exit interview after his failed experiment, he is reported to have said, "I confess that I have committed many faults. I committed them because I am a man, and all men are liable to error; but I declare to you most solemnly that none of them proceeded from wicked or dishonest motives, and that nothing of the kind will be found in the whole course of my conduct."[23]

In the next chapter, we'll introduce his counterpart, Type II charlatan extraordinaire John Blunt, who took the ball from John Law and ran with it, creating perhaps the biggest bubble in recorded history.

Notes

1. Lowenstein R. *America's Bank: The Epic Struggle to Create the Federal Reserve.* New York: Penguin Press; 2015.
2. Balen M. *The king, the Crook, and the Gambler: The True Story of the South Sea Bubble and the Greatest Financial Scandal in History.* New York: Harper Perennial; 2004.
3. Mackay C. *Extraordinary Popular Delusions and the Madness of Crowds: Financial Edition.* Hampshire: Harriman House; 1841.
4. Train J. *Famous Financial Fiascos.* New York: Random House; 1984.
5. Ibid.
6. Mackay C. *Extraordinary Popular Delusions and the Madness of Crowds: Financial Edition.* Hampshire: Harriman House; 1841.
7. The Mississippi bubble. Winton [Internet]. 2019 Apr 29. Available from: https://www.winton.com/longer-view/the-mississippi-bubble
8. Mackay C. *Extraordinary Popular Delusions and the Madness of Crowds: Financial Edition.* Hampshire: Harriman House; 1841.
9. Harari YN. *Sapiens: A Brief History of Humankind.* New York: HarperCollins; 2015.

10. Chancellor E. *Devil Take the Hindmost: A History of Financial Speculation.* New York: Plume; 2000.

11. Taylor B. Government debt (so why can't Bernanke?). Global Financial Data [Internet]. 2013 Oct 9. Available from: http://www.gfdblog.com/GFD/Blog/mississippi-bubble-how-french-eliminated-all-government-debt

12. Train J. *Famous Financial Fiascos.* New York: Random House; 1984.

13. Mackay C. *Extraordinary Popular Delusions and the Madness of Crowds: Financial Edition.* Hampshire: Harriman House; 1841.

14. Chancellor E. *Devil Take the Hindmost: A History of Financial Speculation.* New York: Plume; 2000.

15. Mackay C. *Extraordinary Popular Delusions and the Madness of Crowds: Financial Edition.* Hampshire: Harriman House; 1841.

16. The Mississippi bubble. Winton [Internet]. 2019 Apr 29. Available from: https://www.winton.com/longer-view/the-mississippi-bubble

17. Mackay C. *Extraordinary Popular Delusions and the Madness of Crowds: Financial Edition.* Hampshire: Harriman House; 1841.

18. Balen M. *The king, the Crook, and the Gambler: The True Story of the South Sea Bubble and the Greatest Financial Scandal in History.* New York: Harper Perennial; 2004.

19. Ibid.

20. Train J. *Famous Financial Fiascos.* New York: Random House; 1984.

21. Balen M. *The king, the Crook, and the Gambler: The True Story of the South Sea Bubble and the Greatest Financial Scandal in History.* New York: Harper Perennial; 2004.

22. Mackay C. *Extraordinary Popular Delusions and the Madness of Crowds: Financial Edition.* Hampshire: Harriman House; 1841.

23. Ibid.

CHAPTER

11

Type II Charlatan

In all speculative episodes there is always an element of pride in discovering what is seemingly new and greatly rewarding in the way of financial instrument or investment opportunity.
—John Kenneth Galbraith

Frogs have almost 360-degree vision because their necks can't move much. When a frog's vision works in concert with their appetite it can produce some strange reactions. Put a dead fly on a string and dangle it in front of a hungry frog and it won't eat it. The frog is almost entirely unaware the fly exists. But put a live fly in the same room as a hungry frog and the frog will do everything in its power to pursue its prey. You see a frog's eyesight works in such a way that they can only see certain objects when they're moving. If it's not moving, it doesn't even register to the frog.[1]

Financial markets work much in the same way when it comes to triggering the human brain to pay attention. The slow, methodical, long-term movements in the stock market aren't exciting so it basically registers as a nonevent. It's much easier to notice the high-flying stock or fad investment du jour that moves quickly in the short term. Those quick moves are what cause investors to overreact and make mistakes causing people to make short-term decisions with long-term capital at

121

stake. The biggest difference between us and the frogs is they have more discipline to wait it out when the dead fly is dangling in front of their face than we do. Stability almost acts as its own form of instability in the markets because the human brain craves another hit of dopamine once it experiences a change in the status quo.

This idea that stability can lead to instability was first developed by economist Hyman Minsky. Minsky published *The Financial Instability Hypothesis* in the early 1990s, claiming, "Over periods of prolonged prosperity, the economy transits from financial relations that make for a stable system to financial relations that make for an unstable system."[2]

In non-economist speak, this means a stable financial system eventually tempts investors to borrow money to buy more expensive assets, which leads to the inevitable downturns when investors go overboard. Minsky was basically explaining the idea that markets have cycles that go from periods of stability to periods of instability and back again. But he was also laying out the case for how bubbles occur. People get bored. They take risks they shouldn't take when markets get expensive by borrowing too much money to juice returns. And eventually the music stops and the dance floor empties. Success by an individual can lead to overconfidence. Success by others can lead to envy and regret. Mix overconfidence with envy and regret and you get extreme risk-taking by individuals that collectively become a herd that overwhelms rational thought. This is the Minsky moment.

Robert Shiller defined the idea of a herd mentality in his book *Irrational Exuberance*, which was released at the tail end of the dotcom bubble:

> I define a speculative bubble as a situation in which news of price increases spurs investor enthusiasm, which spreads by psychological contagion from person to person, in the process amplifying stories that might justify the price increases and bringing in a larger and larger class of investors, who, despite doubts about the real value of an investment, are drawn to it partly through envy of others' successes and partly through a gambler's excitement.[3]

Financial writer and investor William Bernstein describes four conditions that are necessary for a bubble, in his book *The Four Pillars of Investing*:

1. A major technological revolution or shift in financial practice.
2. Liquidity – i.e., easy credit.

3. Amnesia for the last bubble. This usually takes a generation.
4. Abandonment of time-honored methods of security valuation, usually caused by the takeover of the market by inexperienced investors.[4]

There's another element that can supercharge a bubble – fraud. Authoritative figures making faulty promises, hiding relevant information, or leaking rumors can add fuel to the fire. The man spraying gasoline all over England during the early part of the eighteenth century was John Blunt, helping create what might be the biggest bubble of all time.

The South Sea Company

Britain and France were at war with one another and other parts of the world for centuries by the time they went to battle on the economic front in the early 1700s. The British government saw what John Law was creating in France with the Mississippi Company to handle the country's war debts. The Brits saw French citizens getting rich overnight by owning shares in a company that was taking on those debts. A combination of jealousy and anxiety caused England to follow Law's lead by using a publicly traded company that could shoulder the debt burden of the country.

England was almost always placing itself in a superior position to other European countries, so government officials and citizens alike felt they deserved the same treatment France was getting on their debt load. Plenty of people assumed Law's monetary plan would fail (see the last chapter: it did) but the Brits assumed it could never happen to them. In fact, Parliament signed off on the South Sea scheme at the height of John Law's Mississippi bubble. It was a race to the finish to see which country could act more delirious.[5]

The South Sea Company used the Mississippi Company's playbook in that it was an exploration business that issued shares to the public in exchange for the government's debt and annuities owned by investors. In exchange for taking on the government's debts, the company was granted a monopoly on trade routes in the South Seas. Everyone heard rumors of endless amounts of gold and silver in places like Peru and Mexico. Investors actually believed these resources were inexhaustible and that all it would take was a handful of ships to bring home untold riches. Let's just say this take didn't age well.

The company started out relatively small, taking over £10 million in debt from the government. But once the government and public collectively grew jealous of John Law's scheme in France, it was time to take it to another level. In 1719, the South Sea Company offered its stock to the public in exchange for Britain's remaining debt load. When the South Sea Company led the first ever secondary stock offering in history, it was hoping to raise £2 million. It raised half of that amount by midmorning. People were pawning their possessions, and farmers were selling livestock to raise cash to buy shares. The offering was oversubscribed.[6]

Company management hoped to increase speculative interest in the stock price to offer less and less of it in exchange for government debt, because debt holders could sell out for an immediate profit. Then the management team could keep the extra stock they helped create. And that's basically what happened. The share price went from 129 to 360 in no time. After the first conversion it went as high as 890.[7] The market cap of the company reached £12 million after becoming a public corporation, yet it still hadn't made a profit. Not only that, it had still not made a single cent on direct trade with South America, which was the entire business plan in the first place.[8]

In the span of around eight months the entire debt structure of the country had been transformed, euphoria gripped the populace, riches were made and subsequently lost, and one man was blamed more than any other – John Blunt.

Type II Charlatan John Blunt

In the last chapter we looked at the difference between Type I and Type II charlatans. Type I charlatans, such as John Law, are the visionaries who are more or less sincere but wind up ruining their investors anyways. They are intellectual frauds because they fail to take into account real-world dynamics or consider how their ideas could go horribly wrong. Type II charlatans are the true fraudsters who blatantly set out to take advantage of others for their own personal gain.

John Blunt was the personification of a Type II charlatan. The man had one aim in life – to become fabulously wealthy by any means necessary. And not only did he want to become rich, he wanted to become rich as fast as humanly possible. Unlike Law, Blunt was no intellectual. But he made up for it through a combination of self-confidence and charisma. Blunt saw an opportunity to use the government, the public, and the South Sea Company to his advantage to both erase government debt and enrich himself in the process.

Blunt was a founding director in the company and described by one account as "burly and overbearing, glib, ingenious, and determined to get on."[9] But Blunt also had an innate ability to get the upper echelon of society on board with his schemes through his sales ability. First he convinced the Prince of Wales to become part of the venture in 1715. Later he talked King George I into becoming a larger shareholder in the company. Even those who are already wealthy and in positions of power can be seduced by get-rich-quick schemes.[10]

As a founding director of the South Sea Company, Blunt had every intention of using its unique corporate structure to personally profit in any way he could. Here's the rap sheet on how Blunt manipulated this situation to his advantage:

- He purchased options on the dividends paid out by the company, dividends he himself planned on raising in short order.
- He secretly increased the number of shares going to himself and his friends.
- He bribed the courts and invested heavily in shares on behalf of friends and family members of Parliament.
- He spread false rumors as far and wide as humanly possible to pump up the stock price.
- He bribed the Secretary of Treasury, Charles Stanhope, with share options (Stanhope later sold his shares during the bubble for enormous profits).
- He followed John Law's lead by pushing investors into borrowed funds to boost the share price. In fact, the South Sea Company itself lent money to investors to buy shares. Blunt simply wanted to flood the market to prop up the share price.

As with the Mississippi experiment, the South Sea debt-for-equity exchange made little sense as a legitimate financial trade. Yet the government loved wiping its books clean of their overbearing debt load, and the people buying the stock loved seeing their net worth increase in a short period of time. Blunt's plan was simultaneously attractive and deceptive, a perfect mix for duping people out of their money. As share prices rose so too did investor profits, but the company still didn't make any money. All he was doing was pulling nonexistent profits forward. The South Sea Company had no business plan and no market for its goods.[11]

Maybe the most absurd aspect of the arrangement was Blunt never bothered to inform investors what the conversion terms were for the national debt nor did investors bother to ask. There was no set exchange rate for converting debt into a company share price. The higher the price went, the less the company would have to hand out in shares, leaving more for Blunt and the other directors to do as they pleased with the leftovers. The goal was to push the price up by any means necessary. The company spent millions on bribes, making Blunt feel untouchable, which is a common symptom among those caught up in a financial mania driven by fraud. And for a time he was, considering he was knighted for his efforts. South Sea shares were *the* topic of conversation among the upper class. At one point the company was valued at 10 times the size of the debt it held because Blunt offered such generous terms to entice people to trade in or buy shares. But the ships had still not taken a single voyage to the South Seas.[12]

Whereas John Law's financial experiment had tried (and failed) to solve that country's debt problem using a paper currency, Blunt's scheme truly had no grounding in reality. There was no plan B other than jacking up the share price as high as humanly possible. As the South Sea Company share price began to pick up steam, Blunt told his fellow directors, "The more confusion the better; People must not know what they do, which will make them the more eager to come into our measures; the execution of the Scheme is our business; the Eyes of all Europe are upon us." And the higher the price of shares, the harder it became to keep the momentum going because eventually you run out of new suckers to invest. When the price of the stock finally began its descent, the majority of investors actually owed more money than their shares were worth because they purchased so much of the investment using borrowed funds.[13]

Blunt's plan for world domination sounded like something straight out of Dr. Evil's playbook in *Austin Powers*. According to Charles Mackay, Blunt said, "that if the plan succeeded, the directors would become masters of the government, form a new and absolute aristocracy in the kingdom, and control the resolutions of the legislature. If it failed, which he was convinced it would, the result would bring general discontent and ruin upon the country." Dr. Evil simply wanted to blow up the planet with a "laser." At least he didn't try to get people's hopes up first.[14]

The Bubble Act

The year 1720 may have ushered in the word "bubble" to the financial lexicon. It was known to some people as the "bubble year." After the success of the South Sea Company in raising funds from investors, joint-stock companies sprang up like weeds. These companies were even called bubbles at the time, which falls under the too-good-to-be-true category of this story. The length of time these companies lasted would make some of the dot-com flameouts in the late-1990s blush. More than 100 new corporations were formed out of nowhere, cashing in on the overwhelming greed, while most lasted no more than a week or two. One company marketed a hydrostatical air pump which would "draw all manner of wind and vapours out of human brains."

The most absurd of these business plans was for a company described as "carrying on an undertaking of great advantage, but nobody to know what it is." For his troubles in this mysterious endeavor, the inventor of said business plan asked for a mere half million pounds. So great was the demand for new public companies, when he set up an office, crowds lined up out the door to the office, which had been set up that very same day. After one thousand shares were sold, the man closed up shop, left the country and was never heard from again. Talk about a get-rich-quick scheme![15]

All of this competition for the greed which had infected the populace meant fewer people paying attention to South Sea shares, so the price began to fall. With the help of his paid-for friends in Parliament, Blunt was able to push through legislation called the Bubble Act, which made it harder to start a new company without prior government approval. This gave the South Sea Company a monopoly on speculation, but the victory was short lived. Once a selling stampede begins there's not much the government can do to stem the tide. After hitting a price of £1,000 in August, shares quickly fell to 150 by September. The company never came close to making a profit and ended up a money-losing venture.[16]

The company's collapse reverberated through Great Britain. Thousands of people went bankrupt. Banks were also out of luck because they couldn't collect the money owed to them by investors because the collateral used for margin accounts was worthless shares in South Sea. No one wanted to blame the speculators themselves. Everyone wanted a scapegoat. Charles Mackay explained:

> Nobody seemed to imagine that the nation itself was as culpable as the South Sea Company. Nobody blamed the credulity and avarice of the people – the degrading lust of gain…or the infatuation which had made the multitude run their heads with such frantic eagerness into the net held out for them by scheming projectors. These things were never mentioned.[17]

Charlatans and hucksters like John Blunt are never going away. There will always be fraudsters that strike the match but it's the crowd psychology that provides the accelerant. No one bothered to perform even the faintest research on the prospects of the company itself. Not a single ship had set sail anywhere close to the South Seas! Blunt was forced to retire in Bath with just £5,000 to his name and all of his other assets confiscated.

The Echo Bubble and Dunbar's Number

For hundreds of thousands of years, our ancestors functioned mainly in small tribes. Life was hard. Each individual had their own job, and in large part everyone was simply trying to survive. One of the reasons these tribes tended to be small is because there is a relationship between the size of our social groups and the size of our brains. As our brains evolved over tens of thousands of years Homo sapiens began to form larger groups through word of mouth, and to some degree, gossip. The upper band of this number is around 150 people according to sociology research.

Dunbar's number is named after the anthropologist Robin Dunbar who theorized that the natural size of a group is about 150 individuals. Dunbar posited that judging by the size of the human brain, this is the number of people the average person can have in their wider social group. This makes sense when you consider most of the weddings you attend have anywhere from 100 to 300 people in attendance. Dunbar discovered the average size of our hunter-gatherer ancestors was roughly 148 individuals.[18]

When social groups were this size, people could only compare themselves to others in their small tribe. Depending on your talents, you were bound to be the best at *something*, but humans were more worried about survival than keeping up with the Joneses. Technology and storytelling have changed all that. Homo sapiens were eventually able to create cities, religions, and companies with thousands and even millions of people through the art of storytelling. Going from hunter-gatherers to an agricultural source of food was the first major shift, while the printing press was the huge technological leap forward that allowed wide dissemination of these stories. The Internet is the printing press on steroids so it feels like it's harder than ever to avoid trying to keep up with your neighbors, peers, friends, coworkers, or fake celebrities on Instagram.

While technology may ramp up our fascination with the Joneses, whoever they may be, you can take some comfort in the fact that the herd mentality has been around since long before likes, retweets, and influencers ruled social media.

Gustave Le Bon was a French psychologist who wrote the book *The Crowd: A Study of the Popular Mind* all the way back in 1895. The passage sums up his findings well:

> The most striking peculiarity presented by a psychological crowd is the following: Whoever be the individuals that compose it, however like or unlike be their mode of life, their occupations, their character, or their intelligence, the fact that they have been transformed into a crowd puts them in possession of a sort of collective mind that makes them feel, think and act in a manner quite different from that in which each individual of them would feel, think and act were he in a state of isolation. There are certain feelings that do not come into being, or do not transform themselves into acts, except in the case of individuals forming a crowd.[19]

This work was written 175 years or so after the South Sea and Mississippi bubbles, but it sounds like it could have been written by a reporter who was on the streets of London or Paris witnessing the madness of the crowds going nuts for those companies. Le Bon's passage would also be relevant to the roaring 20s in the lead-up to the Great Depression, the 1980s property and stock market mania in Japan, the dot-com bubble at the tail end of the 1990s, or the real estate bubble of the 2000s.

The markets, countries, and people change but the herd mentality is the one constant in all these situations. Once we surpassed Dunbar's number and created modern society beyond the tribes of our ancestors, these situations became inevitable. Our brains simply aren't hardwired to watch someone else get rich quickly if we're not joining in the fun. This makes financial bubbles unavoidable. It also means Type II charlatans will always be there waiting to take advantage.

Notes

1. Arbesman S. *The Half Life of Facts: Why Everything We Know Has an Expiration Date.* New York: Penguin Group; 2012.
2. Minsky HP. The financial instability hypothesis. Levy Economics Institute of Bard College, Working Paper No. 74. Available from: http://www.levyinstitute.org/pubs/wp74.pdf
3. Shiller RJ. *Irrational Exuberance.* Princeton, New Jersey: Princeton University Press; 2000.
4. Bernstein WJ. *The Four Pillars of Investing: Lessons for Building a Winning Portfolio.* New York: McGraw-Hill; 2010.
5. Mackay C. *Extraordinary Popular Delusions and the Madness of Crowds: Financial Edition.* Hampshire: Harriman House; 1841.
6. Carswell J. *The South Sea Bubble.* London: The Cresset Press; 1960.
7. Train J. *Famous Financial Fiascos.* New York: Random House; 1984.
8. Balen M. *The King, the Crook, and the Gambler: The True Story of the South Sea Bubble and the Greatest Financial Scandal in History.* New York: Harper Perennial; 2004.
9. Carswell J. *The South Sea Bubble.* London: The Cresset Press; 1960.
10. Balen M. *The King, the Crook, and the Gambler: The True Story of the South Sea Bubble and the Greatest Financial Scandal in History.* New York: Harper Perennial; 2004.
11. Ibid.
12. Ibid.
13. Balen M. *The Secret History of the South Sea Bubble: The World's First Great Financial Scandal.* New York: Harper; 2003.
14. Mackay C. *Extraordinary Popular Delusions and the Madness of Crowds: Financial Edition.* Hampshire: Harriman House; 1841.
15. Ibid.
16. Taylor B. Complete histories – the South Seas Company – the forgotten ETC. Global Financial Data [Internet] 2013 Aug 21. Available from: http://www.gfdblog.com/GFD/Blog/gfd-complete-histories-south-seas-company-the-forgotten-etf
17. Mackay C. *Extraordinary Popular Delusions and the Madness of Crowds: Financial Edition.* Hampshire: Harriman House; 1841.
18. Dunbar R. Is there a limit to how many friends we can have? TED Radio Hour, National Public Radio [Internet]. 2017 Jan 13. Available from: https://www.npr.org/2017/01/13/509358157/is-there-a-limit-to-how-many-friends-we-can-have
19. Le Bon G. *The Crowd: A Study of the Popular Mind.* 1895.

CHAPTER 12

Fooled by Intelligence

*I guarantee that in every great blow-up there has been at least one
big name investor involved all the way down.*

—Jim Chanos

On May 25, 1961, President John F. Kennedy stood before Congress with an audacious goal, proclaiming, "this nation should commit itself to achieving the goal, before the decade is out, of landing a man on the moon and returning him safely to the earth."

NASA analysts put those chances at 1 in 10 of ever happening. Neil Armstrong and his fellow astronauts on the Apollo 11 mission would never have achieved that goal in 1969 had it not been for the crew of the Apollo 8. This less well-known mission occurred during Christmas time in 1968 and included the crew who were the first to ever orbit the moon. Armstrong's famous first steps on the moon have overshadowed the first lunar orbit but, in many ways, this earlier mission may have been more impressive and riskier. Not only had it never been done before, but NASA was racing against the Russians to get there first, had little time to fully test all of their systems, and had no idea if their plans and calculations would actually hold up if the spaceship ever got there.

The crew on the spaceship – Frank Borman, Jim Lovell (the astronaut Tom Hanks played in the movie *Apollo 13*), and Bill Anders – faced daunting odds. The Apollo 8 spacecraft was built using 5.6 million parts and 1.5 million systems, subsystems, and assemblies. Assuming a 99.9% effective rate, that would mean they could expect to see 5,600 defects along the way. Charles Lindbergh calculated Apollo 8 would burn more fuel in the first second of flight than he did on his entire trip on the first-ever nonstop flight across the Atlantic. That amount of fuel had the explosive power of a small nuclear bomb. To achieve orbit outside the gravitational pull of earth, Apollo 8 would need to be traveling more than 17,000 miles per hour. On re-entry into the earth's atmosphere, the ship would be traveling almost 25,000 mph.

Roughly 39,000 miles from the moon is a point called equigravisphere, where the pull of gravity is equal between the earth and the moon. Passing this point would make Borman, Lovell, and Anders the first people to ever be captured by a gravitational pull outside of our own planet's. To fly around the other side of the moon, a place no person's eyes had ever seen before, required 240,000 miles of travel. The moon itself would move 150,000 miles in the time it took for the spacecraft to get there.

The biggest test would come when Apollo 8 reached the far side of the moon. At that point, the ship would lose radio contact. Frank Borman, the commander of the flight, was fixated on this moment in the months leading up to takeoff. NASA calculated the orientation of the spaceship in the flight plan by aligning themselves with the stars through what's called sextant sightings. This was similar to the system sailing ships used for centuries, executed by measuring the angles between the sun, the moon, and the stars. NASA specialists who planned the flight would calculate the spaceship's altitude based on its position relative to different stars and use the thrusters to keep its position in the desired location. Any calculated change in velocity would let the crew and mission control know if they were on course or made a grievous error.

If radio contact was lost for too long, it meant the ship was traveling too fast and was off course. If they lost radio contact too early, it meant orbit was off. If either of these scenarios came to pass the astronauts would likely be lost in space forever as they wouldn't have the fuel required to fight the gravitational pull of the moon to make it home.

Robert Kurson explained what happened at this pivotal moment in his riveting book, *Rocket Men: The Daring Odyssey of Apollo 8 and the Astronauts Who Made Man's First Journey to the Moon*:

> Borman's stomach tightened.
> Lovell and Anders stared at the clock.
> The view out the windows became even darker.
> The astronauts' headsets went silent.
> Borman looked at the clock.
> "Jeez," he said.
> Radio contact had been lost at precisely the second NASA had calculated.
> Borman could hardly believe it. Anders joked, "Chris [Kraft] probably said, 'No matter what happens, turn it off.'"
> Anders had seen how concerned – obsessed – Borman had been about this moment during training. It took a second for Borman to realize Anders was kidding. After that, Borman couldn't stop smiling. Another critical hurdle in the Apollo 8 mission had been cleared.
> In Houston, controllers looked at each other with a sense of wonder and relief, shaking their heads and then shaking hands. Orbital mechanics – the way the universe ordered and moved itself – worked. And man had figured it out to the split second.

When the ship finished its first orbit around the far side of the moon the astronauts came back into radio contact within one second of NASA's estimate. NASA had calculated the dimensions of the orbit of the moon to within a fraction of a mile. After making it around the moon and using its gravitational pull as something of a slingshot to send them back, the astronauts were on their way home on Christmas day. Some of the crew had their families at NASA headquarters in Houston. The five-year-old son of a crew member at mission control asked Bill Anders who was driving the ship. "That's a good question," Anders replied. "I think Isaac Newton is doing most of the driving right now."[1]

Anders was referring to the laws of math and physics that were developed by Sir Isaac Newton in the seventeenth century. The beauty of these laws is they allowed scientists at NASA to accurately measure where and when Apollo 8 would hit certain checkpoints along its journey through outerspace. In a roundabout way, having an accurate model of the universe allowed NASA to predict the future. Unfortunately, the position of the planets provides a much simpler model for prediction than the financial markets for the simple fact that human emotions are not governed by the laws of physics. When dealing with complex adaptive systems such as financial markets, it's impossible to predict the future because of the human variable, something Newton himself would come to learn firsthand.

Newton's Mania

Isaac Newton's contributions in mathematics, astronomy, physics, alchemy, theology, engineering, and technology make him arguably the most important figure of the scientific revolution. Not only was the man a world-renowned scientist, he also took part in debates on monetary policy within the government and helped pursue counterfeiters in his work with the Royal Mint. Newton died a rich man as his life's work paid well but no one remembers how much money Newton made or squirreled away. The only story anyone knows about Sir Newton when it comes to money matters was his experience losing a boatload of cash investing in the aforementioned South Sea bubble.

Newton is widely attributed with the quote, "I can calculate the motion of heavenly bodies, but not the madness of people," after losing his shirt in South Sea Company shares. This is the chef's kiss of behavioral finance quotes. It's been used countless times because it makes the perfect point that even one of the smartest people on the planet can succumb to his emotions when money is involved. Unfortunately, Newton likely never said the first part of the quote. He is on record responding to a question about the ever-rising price of the South Sea stock price by saying, "I could not calculate the madness of the people," but the "calculate the motion of the heavenly bodies" part was likely added in later by other writers to beef up the narrative. Regardless of where the entirety of the quote originated, Newton's experience is still worth revisiting because investing in the South Sea Company provides lessons for the rest of us who will never be one of the most influential minds in recorded history.

Newton died a wealthy man with an estate valued at roughly £30,000, but lost anywhere from £10,000 to £20,000 from his foray into the beast that was the South Sea bubble. That £20,000 would be the equivalent of roughly £20 million today. By all accounts, Newton was a conservative, shrewd, and successful investor before the South Sea stock caught his fancy, investing prudently in mostly stocks and government bonds.[2]

The South Sea Company was an innovative experiment at the outset so the fact that Newton was an early investor makes him something of a venture capital pioneer. He began buying up shares in 1712, just a year after it was incorporated, and a full seven to eight years before the madness of the crowds took the price to the stratosphere. Newton saw some nice gains in his trading account on the initial price surge and proved to be a momentum trader by making six more purchases as the price continued to rise. A majority of those purchases were at prices higher than where he ended up selling out but he was still able to take some gains and nearly double his initial investment. Yet after he sold the price kept right on rising as the bubble really took off after his cash was on the sidelines.

To quote Al Pacino in *The Godfather, Part III*, "Just when I thought I was out, they pull me back in!" The ever-rising share price sucked Newton in hook, line, and sinker. After selling out of his entire stake, Newton would jump back in just a few short weeks later at double the price he sold. It was a panic buy, most likely caused by greed's best friend, the fear of missing out. FOMO quickly turned into the fear of being in, as Newton was looking at a loss of nearly 80% on his capital by the end of 1723.

Researchers believe Newton is the only large investor who initially took profits on his investment in the South Sea Company, only to jump back in at a later date and lose the bulk of his money.[3]

For the rest of his life Newton claimed he couldn't bear to mention the name of the company that caused him such grief and losses.[4] John Blunt's pump-and-dump of massive proportions had snagged one of the most intelligent people to ever walk the earth.

The Problem with Smartest People in the Room

Bethany McLean was a reporter for *Fortune* when she shed light on the Enron fraud in 2001. The Houston-based energy company used a variety of deception and fraudulent accounting practices that masked the true performance of the business. McLean described one of the largest corporate frauds in history in her book about the subject, *The Smartest Guys in the Room,* quoting an employee who explained how the company's financial shenanigans generally worked:

> Say you have a dog, but you need to create a duck on the financial statements. Fortunately, there are specific accounting rules

for what constitutes a duck: yellow feet, white covering, orange beak. So you take the dog and paint its feet yellow and its fur white and you paste an orange plastic beak on its nose, and then you say to your accountants, 'This is a duck! Don't you agree that it's a duck?' And the accountants say, 'Yes, according to the rules, this is a duck.' Everybody knows that it's a dog, not a duck, but that doesn't matter, because you've met the rules for calling it a duck.

Company management overstated profits by roughly $600 million while assets were overstated by $24 billion using shady mark-to-market accounting techniques. Prior to declaring the largest bankruptcy in US history up to that point in time, Enron was the seventh largest corporation by revenue. Enron was named "the most innovative company" six years running from 1995–2000, right before they blew up. They were also named the seventh "most admired" company in 2001, the very same year they declared bankruptcy.

In her book, McLean profiles former Enron CEO Jeffrey Skilling, who was eventually sentenced to 24 years in prison for his role in the fraud:

> When people describe Skilling they don't just use the word "smart"; they use phrases like "incandescently brilliant" or "the smartest person I ever met." Skilling in the late 1980s wasn't a physically striking man – he was smallish, a little pudgy, and balding – but his mental agility was breathtaking. He could process information and conceptualize new ideas with blazing speed. He could instantly simplify complex issues into a sparkling, compelling image. And he presented his ideas with a certainty that bordered on arrogance and brooked no dissent. He used his brain power not just to persuade but to intimidate.[5]

Unfortunately for the thousands of Enron employees who lost an estimated $850 million investing in the company's stock, Skilling used his incandescent brilliance for deception. The problem with brilliance is that it can lead to blind spots. Every human on the planet has a lesser version of themselves. Even the most skilled among us have deficiencies in other areas of life. It's just that it's often much easier to see the irrationalities in others than ourselves. There are hundreds of documented cognitive biases we as a species are prone to, but the hardest one to wrap your head around is the blind spot bias. This is the idea that it's much easier to see bias in others than yourself. And intelligent people are prone to this issue more than anyone because they become so good at self-deception.

Researchers Richard West, Russell Meserve, and Keith Stanovich performed a variety of studies that confirm this idea. Not only did they find an inherent blind spot bias through their research, but they found an even bigger blind spot towards biases from those with higher cognitive abilities. After testing for seven cognitive abilities, these researchers concluded, "In addition, cognitive ability did not attenuate this metacognitive bias. Furthermore, people who were aware of their own biases were not better able to overcome them." Said another way, smarter people may be worse off than others at recognizing their own limitations. This makes sense when you realize intelligent people have more firepower to convince themselves that they must be right about most things, simply because they are smarter than the average person.[6]

Why Smart People Make Dumb Decisions

John Kenneth Galbraith once wrote, "Fools, as it has long been said, are indeed separated, soon or eventually from their money." But are the fools really the only ones who get taken? Is it just the poor schmucks who are willingly handing their money over to hucksters and fraudsters? In a word – no. Intelligent people have no problem making irrational choices with their money.

A high income, large portfolio, diploma from a prestigious university, or envious job title do not automatically qualify you to become successful at managing money. In fact, many of the worst investors are highly successful in other fields. That success can lead to your downfall when it comes to managing a business or money if you're not careful.

In a roundtable discussion following a visit to Theranos in 2015, Vice President Joe Biden stated he had just witnessed, "the laboratory of the future." Theranos is the Silicon Valley healthcare company that promised it could take a pinprick of blood from a patient's fingertip to run a series of diagnostics that would revolutionize the blood-testing process. The company was famously founded by Elizabeth Holmes, who dropped out of Stanford at age 19 to create a device that, according to her, was "the most important thing humanity has ever built." The Holmes story was the perfect Silicon Valley fairy tale, destined to become a best-selling business book and movie. Sadly, this fairy tale turned out to be more of a horror flick, for patients and investors alike.

The chutzpah of Holmes to even invite Biden to take a tour of the facilities is next level considering the entire company was a fraud. The lab Holmes showed Biden was staged. The devices didn't actually work. The majority of the lab workers were told to stay home that day. Holmes even faked the inflection of her voice, making it much deeper than it actually was in an attempt to sound more serious. Biden was far from the only big name to be conned by Holmes.[7]

Her story was so convincing she managed to fool a who's who of the wealthy elite. The Walton family, heirs to the Walmart fortune, lost $150 million. Media mogul Rupert Murdoch put $125 million into the company based strictly on gut feel alone for due diligence purposes. He would later sell the entire stake for $1 to take a tax write-off for the enormous loss on a worthless investment. Betsy DeVos, the Education Secretary for President Trump, and her wealthy family lost $100 million. The list of investors also included New England Patriots owner Robert Kraft, Mexican billionaire Carlos Slim, and a Greek shipping magnate. Partner Fund Management, a well-known hedge fund, purchased shares at a valuation that pegged the company's value at $9 billion. On paper, that made Holmes worth a staggering $5 billion.[8]

It never occurred to these investors that anything out of the ordinary could be going on with this company because of the prestigious names involved with the project. The Theranos board was overflowing with big names. There was former US Defense Secretary Jim Mattis, former Secretary of State George Shultz, retired US Navy Admiral Gary Roughead, former Secretary of State Henry Kissinger, and former Secretary of Defense William Perry. Shultz, the man many credit with helping win the Cold War, anointed Holmes as, "the next Steve Jobs or Bill Gates." Instead Holmes orchestrated one of the biggest frauds ever, fooling some of the richest investors and well-connected aristocrats around.

Fooling Yourself with Complexity

Successful people can fall prey to such grievous financial errors because it's easier to personalize your successes once you've reached a certain status in life. Brendan Moynihan tells the story of Jim Paul in his book, *What I Learned Losing a Million Dollars*. As you might guess from the title, Paul's story is about making, then losing, a lot of money in a short amount of time. Moynihan learned from Paul that, "Personalizing successes sets people up for disastrous failure. They begin to treat the successes totally as a personal reflection of their abilities rather than the result of capitalizing on a good opportunity, being at the right place at the right time, or even being just plain lucky. They think their mere involvement in an undertaking guarantees success." When you have money, name recognition, celebrity, or power it can make you feel invincible. But everyone can be swindled out of their money, whether they made it through hard work, luck, or a combination of the two.

Too much intelligence can be a dangerous thing as it can leave you susceptible to overthinking things and becoming overconfident in your own abilities. And when others around you assume intelligence is the be-all, end-all, no one else holds you accountable for your decisions. Unchecked intelligence is the worst kind because you begin to believe you're unstoppable. Money doesn't care what your IQ is, which is why emotional intelligence and temperament are more important than your SAT scores. Enron was led by brilliant business minds, but those leaders lacked common sense, self-awareness, humility, and a moral compass. Talent is overrated in the business world if it doesn't include people skills.

Everyone makes mistakes when it comes to their finances because no one knows exactly how the future will play out. Some fields allow practitioners the ability to work with an extreme level of precision, even in the face of uncertainty. Finance is not one of those fields. You can't calculate relationships in the markets like you can the distance between the stars. Retirement planning, portfolio management, investment strategies, and personal finance are all forms of guesswork in many ways.

You're forced to deal with uncertainty, but you don't have a perfect model that allows you to calculate your exact position in relation to your goal. Planning out your financial future is like trying to calculate orbital mechanics while the stars are constantly moving, changing shape, or disappearing for good. Like the astronauts on Apollo 8, you must make occasional course corrections. But unlike the heroes who went to the moon and back, you can't tell if those course corrections are helping or hurting right away. Therefore, a process is required to keep you on track if you ever wish to achieve your financial goals.

The biggest thing you can do to keep your sanity and finances in order in the face of this irreducible uncertainty is to become process-oriented with your finances. Being process-oriented means:

- Never prescribing a solution before first diagnosing the problem.
- Having strong opinions, weakly held.
- Realizing that short-term tactics are useless without a long-term comprehensive financial plan.
- Understanding what you'll do ahead of time by making good decisions in advance and automating those decisions.
- Admitting the stuff you don't know and recognizing your weak spots.
- Remaining humble, especially when things are going well, because no one knows how long success will last.

Certainties when it comes to your life or your finances are few. The first step in the process is focusing on the intersection of things that are important to you and the things you can control.

Notes

1. Kurson R. *Rocket Men: The Daring Odyssey of Apollo 8 and the Astronauts Who Made Man's First Journey to the Moon.* New York: Random House; 2018.
2. Odlyzko A. Newton's financial misadventures in the South Sea bubble. SSRN [Internet]. 2018 Feb 10. doi: http://dx.doi.org/10.2139/ssrn.3068542
3. Ibid.
4. Balen M. *The king, the Crook, and the Gambler: The True Story of the South Sea Bubble and the Greatest Financial Scandal in History.* New York: Harper Perennial; 2004.
5. McLean B and Elkind P. *The Smartest Guys in the Room: The Amazing Rise and Scandalous Fall of Enron.* New York: Portfolio-Penguin; 2003.
6. West RF, Meserve RJ, and Stanovich KE. Cognitive sophistication does not attenuate the bias blind spot. *Journal of Personality and Social Psychology.* 2012 Sep;103(3):506–19. doi: 10.1037/a0028857
7. Carreyrou J. *Bad blood: Secrets and Lies in a Silicon Valley Startup.* New York: Knopf Doubleday Publishing Group; 2018.
8. Carreyrou J. Theranos cost business and government leaders more than $600 million. *The Wall Street Journal* [Internet]. 2018 May 3. Available from: https://www.wsj.com/articles/theranos-cost-business-and-government-leaders-more-than-600-million-1525392082

13

How Gullible Are You?

The man who is admired for the ingenuity of his larceny is almost always rediscovering some earlier form of fraud.
—John Kenneth Galbraith

Jason Statham has appeared in over 40 major motion pictures, which have grossed upwards of $1 billion in ticket sales. The British actor has a penchant for action movies, appearing in a handful of the *Fast & Furious* movies, *The Expendables* franchise, and a plethora of other films with extended fight scenes, car chases, and stuff getting blown up. I'm partial to his early work in his roles as Turkish in *Snatch* and Bacon in *Lock, Stock and Two Smoking Barrels*, both Guy Ritchie movies, but movie fans obviously enjoy his work.

While Statham is known as an action movie star, he is most certainly not known for reaching out to fans of his movies on Facebook and asking them for money. A woman in England told the BBC she lost a fortune after being contacted on a *Fast & Furious* fan page on the social media site by a man claiming to be Statham. The two sent hundreds of messages back and forth to over the next several months, leading the woman to believe she'd built a solid relationship with the well-known movie star.

So when he told her he was having financial difficulties, claiming he needed a bridge loan until a movie paycheck cleared, she was more than happy to help out by sending cash his way. The woman made a series of payments that cost her hundreds of thousands of pounds. Of course, the person she was talking to online was not Jason Statham. The authorities never were able to track down who defrauded this poor woman but they think it was someone from overseas.[1]

I know what you're thinking: *How could someone be this gullible?!* It seems beyond the realm of possibilities that a bona fide movie star would ever befriend random strangers on the Internet, only to later ask them for money once an online relationship is established. Unfortunately, we're all gullible in our own way.

Psychologist Stephen Greenspan is an expert on human gullibility and why we're so easily persuaded into believing things that just aren't true. Greenspan says a gullible outcome is the result of the interaction between four factors:

1. *The Situation.* Certain situations can exert tremendous tremendous social pressure from family, friends, or the investing public to act. Peer pressure is how bull markets and seemingly good ideas turn into manias, forcing people to jump into the fray even when it seemingly makes no sense.
2. *Cognitive Processes.* Everyone has their own blind spots. For some that means not knowing enough to make an informed financial decision. For others that means becoming overconfident in their ability to pick winning investments. Still others can't see the obvious fraud that's staring them right in the face because they want so badly to believe it's true.
3. *Personality.* Some people are impulsive with their money. They'll spend more time researching the reviews for a $7 purchase on Amazon than they will when making $50,000 investments with their life savings. Others are far too trusting when it comes to money matters.
4. *Emotional State.* Emotions are neither good nor bad; they just are and they make us human. But your emotional state when making big-time decisions can impact your ability to see things clearly. This is especially true when dealing with important financial decisions.

Greenspan penned an entire book on the subject called *The Annals of Gullibility: Why We Get Duped and How to Avoid It.* He explains gullibility is not only the tendency to be duped or taken advantage of but a "pattern of being duped, which repeats itself in different settings, even in the face of warning signs." In the introduction to the book Greenspan listed personal reasons for writing such a book beyond sharing his research with the world at large, admitting he himself was "unusually gullible as a child, and still continue[s] to have gullible moments as an adult."

The Annals of Gullibility was released in December 2008 during the height of the Great Financial Crisis, the worst economic meltdown since the Great Depression. The US stock market fell nearly 40% in 2008 alone. As is the case with many of the frauds profiled throughout this book, when the rug got pulled out from under the markets and the economy was in the toilet, all sorts of financial frauds and charlatans came to light that had been masked for years. There is no greater fraud or charlatan in modern financial history than Bernard L. Madoff. Madoff swindled banks, hedge funds, wealthy investors, celebrities, and charities with his $65 billion Ponzi scheme, which finally came crumbling down that very same December after decades of lies and deceit.

There were plenty of big-name investors who were fooled by Madoff's scheme – Steven Spielberg's foundation; actors Kevin Bacon, Kyra Sedgwick, and John Malkovich; hall of fame pitcher Sandy Koufax; *Forrest Gump* screenwriter Eric Roth; talk show host Larry King; movie producer Jeffrey Katzenberg; and New York Mets' owner Fred Wilpon.[2]

Oh yeah, there was one more person of interest who was invested in Madoff's fund – our gullibility expert Stephen Greenspan. That's right, the guy who literally wrote the book on how gullible we are as a species was a victim of the biggest Ponzi scheme in history, losing a substantial amount of his retirement savings in the process. Greenspan's life's work on the subject just so happened to be released the very same month Madoff's fraud fell apart. Truth really is stranger than fiction sometimes.

In the things-that-did-not-age-well section of his book, Greenspan concluded, "Because gullibility resistance increases as a function of wisdom acquired in the course of human experience, I am optimistic about my own, and others' ability to become less gullible. As one accumulates experience with people, their schemes, and their

foibles, one can acquire the ability to recognize some idea or proposed action as possibly unwise. The ability to hold off being influ-
enced by someone selling a false notion is an ability that can, I think,
increase with age and experience. Obviously, that will not always be
the case, especially where there is cognitive impairment or where
the social pressure is too great or where a scheme calls forth a strong
emotion (such as greed) or where the victim has a personality in
which dysfunctional schemas are too entrenched and where there is,
consequently, an inability to learn from past mistakes."[3]

Many people at the time used Greenspan as a punch line for how
gullible people can be with their finances and it does make for quite
the narrative. But he was generous enough after the fact to share his
story about how even an expert on getting duped could himself get
caught up in the biggest Ponzi scheme ever concocted. Greenspan
was a good sport about the whole ordeal in what must have been a
difficult time for him both professionally and financially. In a piece
he penned for the *Wall Street Journal* shortly after this became public,
he explained:

> In my own case, the decision to invest in the Rye fund reflect-
> ed both my profound ignorance of finance, and my somewhat
> lazy unwillingness to remedy that ignorance. To get around my
> lack of financial knowledge and my lazy cognitive style around
> finance, I had come up with the heuristic (or mental shorthand)
> of identifying more financially knowledgeable advisers and trust-
> ing in their judgment and recommendations. This heuristic had
> worked for me in the past and I had no reason to doubt that it
> would work for me in this case.[4]

Greenspan also cited trust as one of the biggest issues in why so
many chose to invest with Madoff. A close family friend who was an
advisor seemed trustworthy enough and came highly recommended.
The guy was likeable, persuasive, and had even put the majority of
his own net worth into Madoff's fund, which sold Greenspan on the
investment. Other investors shared their positive experiences with
the advisor and the fund. So when a friend warned him that something seemed off about this investment opportunity, Greenspan assumed this detractor was merely being cynical. Certainly the performance numbers for Madoff's fund seemed too good to be true, but
too good to be true tends to work better when thinking about others,
not ourselves. *Nah those numbers are too good to be true. But what if they*

aren't? Why shouldn't I be the one to discover the secret sauce, the Holy Grail, the easy road to riches? I deserve this.

Greenspan wrote, "While as a rule I tend to be a skeptic about claims that seem too good to be true, the chance to invest in a Madoff-run fund was one case where a host of factors – situational, cognitive, personality and emotional – came together to cause me to put my critical faculties on the shelf." Money has a way of clouding the brain and putting all of our critical faculties on the shelf when we start adding up the potential returns in our head. We all think we're special and deserving of extraordinary investment opportunities.

Psychologists call this the Barnum effect. Studies performed in the 1940s and 1970s had experimenters in white lab coats administer personality tests and then hand the subjects a report afterwards to show them their results. What the subjects didn't realize is every report was exactly the same, regardless of the personality test scores. The fake reports contained a long list of results about underlying character, personality traits, and behavioral makeup. Next these subjects were asked to comment on the accuracy of the reports. They were asked to rate the accuracy of the results on a scale of 1 to 5. The average score of was 4.3. Not only were the personality test results made up, Bertram Forer, the researcher who performed the original test, said he put together the reports from a series of horoscopes and astrology readings. So everyone assumed they received unique personality results, but the reports were so generalized they applied to nearly everyone who read them. This is why people believe their horoscopes are eerily accurate. It's not voodoo but common sense. It's also why your own assessment of yourself can be wildly inaccurate at times.[5]

Self-deception becomes even more effortless when groupthink is at play. We often look to others to figure out what the correct behavior should be, especially when dealing with financial matters. We follow the crowd or the narratives instead of what the evidence or common sense would dictate. It feels more comfortable to go along with the crowd when making tough decisions because we look to others during times of uncertainty. When we see other people making profits that's a green light in our brains that we deserve some of those winnings. Other people making money almost always make it seem too good to pass up. One of the main reasons we humans fall for this stuff time and time again is we fail to understand the sacred relationship between risk and reward.

Ponzi versus Bernie

Bernie Madoff ran a pyramid scheme, paying out legacy investors in his fund using cash inflows from new investors. As we learned earlier in the book about the airplane game, this is the type of strategy that works until it doesn't because you need an endless supply of new investors to keep the house of cards standing. Maybe the most impressive (or saddest) thing about the whole Madoff scandal is the fact that it was ever able to grow to the size that it did at $65 billion. The size and scope of his deception makes me wonder: If it wasn't for a certain Italian-born scam artist in the 1920s, might we call the kind of scam Bernie pulled off the Madoff scheme from now on?

I would be remiss if I spent an entire book discussing the history of financial scams without mentioning the godfather of the genre who has the honor of having his very own fraudulent strategy bear his surname. Madoff actually started out his career in a legitimate way, but Charles Ponzi began as a lowly con man forging checks in Canada. This led to a short prison stint that didn't reform the man but made him an even better scam artist. After serving time in the clink Ponzi discovered a system that allowed people to purchase coupons that could be used to buy stamps in other countries. Because currencies can fluctuate wildly from country to country Ponzi saw an opportunity to use these coupons to profit. The idea was to buy stamps in a country with a collapsing currency and redeem them in a country with a strong currency. Buying up a bunch of these stamps at wholesale could lead to a huge profit, assuming you could actually pull off this trade and time it correctly.[6] To make the business sound legitimate, Ponzi claimed to have a network of buyers throughout Europe to facilitate the trades.[7]

Despite his shady financial background, Ponzi opened up a firm called the Securities and Exchange Company to raise money from investors. The pitch to clients was just a tad ambitious. Prospective investors were promised 40% on their original investment after just 90 days! That's not bad considering the prevailing interest rate at the time was just 5%. Forty percent every three months would be an annualized return of almost 285%. Earning 57 times the risk-free interest rate is a pretty good deal if you can get it. Even more investors gave Ponzi money when he upped the ante by offering 90-day notes that would double your money or 50-day paper that would give investors a 50% return on investment.[8]

Once he paid off his first round of investors, people were hooked and the news spread as far and wide as a Kim Kardashian Instagram post. Ponzi was pleasantly surprised to find around 40,000 people sent him money to the tune of $15 million. And most of these initial investors didn't require a withdrawal because so many of them simply rolled their "profits" into another investment with their financial mad scientist.[9] People entrusted a 34-year-old ex-con with millions of dollars based on false promises alone. The 1920s were such a magical time people believed almost anything. Investors ranged from rich politicians to poor immigrants to a priest.[10]

So much money poured in Ponzi barely knew what to do with it, considering his stamp scheme never had a snowball's chance in hell of working. Cash and banknotes piled up from floor to ceiling as naive "investors" assumed they could earn the easiest money on the planet. Ponzi was forced to hire six clerks just to help him keep track of all the money that came in. There was so much cash they had to store it in trash baskets. Because the scheme he purported to run was never realistic in the first place, all this cash made Ponzi fabulously wealthy. He hired a car and chauffeur and walked around town with a gold-tipped cigarette holder.[11]

Luckily, not everyone was so entranced by Ponzi's promises of free money. The *Boston Post* did the math on his stamp idea and realized it was impossible to pull off at scale using some simple back-of-the-envelope math. There weren't enough coupons in existence to pull off Ponzi's claims. After reading the story an angry mob showed up at the SEC offices demanding their money back. Initially, everyone was paid with interest, as Ponzi assured investors there was nothing to worry about (which is exactly what a charlatan would say). He claimed the newspapers didn't know what they were talking about and that he had *another* secret way of making money. The original plan was merely a decoy. The crowd relented and actually handed the huckster even more money that day.

Finally the district attorney stepped in, demanding an audit of his books, which led to a run on the pyramid scheme. Things got so bad the glass door to his office broke and people were injured. The next week the papers interviewed a former partner of Ponzi's who said the con man was "as crooked as a winding staircase" and in debt to the tune $4 million. Reporters also asked why Ponzi put his own money in 5% bank deposits if his strategy was making 50% every 45 days? Why wouldn't he eat his own cooking if it was so good? Such

was the man's hubris that he actually blamed the banks and tried to
sue the newspapers. Finally, someone tracked down a mug shot from
Ponzi's lowly con artist days in Canada just as the auditors revealed
the entire operation was a sham.

Ponzi never even bothered buying the stamp coupons in the first
place, instead paying off legacy investors with new money that was
flowing in. Somehow the operation was still an estimated $3–7 mil-
lion in the hole. Ponzi went back to jail but spent less than four
years behind bars before heading to Florida to give it one more try,
where he was almost immediately sentenced to jail for real estate
fraud. This time he promised 200% to investors in just 60 days. He
was eventually deported back to Italy, where he lived out his life in a
state of poverty.[12]

The Sacred Relationship

Every successful investor must understand there is a sacred relationship between risk and reward. There is no proven way to earn a high
return on your capital without taking some form of risk nor is it possible to completely extinguish risk from your investments. At best
you can trade one risk for another because it never really goes away.
From 1928 through 2018 the US stock market returned 9.5% annu-
ally. That's good enough to double your money every seven to eight
years. Ten-year treasuries, bonds issued and guaranteed by the US
government, returned 4.8% per year over this same time. Cash, as
proxied by three-month US treasury bills, returned 3.4%.

In the hierarchy of asset classes, stocks should return more than
bonds and bonds should return more than cash over the long haul.
Of course this isn't always the case depending on how you define
"long-term," but this should be your baseline for setting expectations. However, investing in the stock market is not free money. You
have to pay your tuition to earn those higher returns. Although the
long-term returns have been in the 9 to 10% range, the annual returns are rarely close to those long-term averages.

In fact, in the 91 years from 1928–2018, there were a grand total
of three years where the market finished a calendar year with returns in the 9 to 11% range. Stocks tend to earn higher long-term
returns than bonds or cash because (a) they can be highly volatile in
the short term and (b) they have a higher risk of large losses. When
stocks are up in a given year, they're typically up big, and when stocks

are down in a given year, they're typically down big. The S&P 500 has experienced positive returns in 66 years since 1928, meaning it was down in the 25 remaining years. When the stock market was up, the average return was close to 21%. And when it was down, the average return was close to negative 13%.

Double-digit returns are the norm in the stock market. Of those 66 positive annual returns, almost 80% of the gains were double-digit up years while almost half were gains of 20% or higher. Almost half of all down years saw double-digit losses while six calendar years experienced losses in excess of 20%. On the other hand, bonds were down in just 18% of all calendar years, meaning they saw positive returns roughly four out of every five years. And the worst loss for 10-year treasuries was just 11% in a single year. The stock market has been down more than 30% in three different years. Cash has never had a down year.

Why am I telling you all of this? Because any investor needs to understand that volatility and losses are the price of admission if you wish to earn higher returns on your money. If you crave safety and stability, you're going to be forced to accept lower returns, or take much greater risks than you realize to earn those stable returns in cash-like investments. Risk and reward are attached at the hip, and anyone who tries to skirt this relationship is almost sure to end up regretting that decision.

Ponzi went straight for the jugular by preying on the greed that existed in the 1920s, but Bernie Madoff never promised outlandish returns. Instead, Madoff focused on our inherent aversion to loss and volatility. Our resident gullibility expert Stephen Greenspan explains:

> A big part of Mr. Madoff's success came from his apparent recognition that wealthy investors were looking for small but steady returns, high enough to be attractive but not so high as to arouse suspicion. This was certainly one of the things that attracted me to the Madoff scheme, as I was looking for a non-volatile investment that would enable me to preserve and gradually build wealth in down as well as up markets.[13]

The markets are controlled by two main emotional responses: fear and greed. Ponzi clearly went for the latter by marketing to the seemingly endless supply of greed that existed at the onset of the roaring 20s. There will always be a market for suckers who get taken in by get-rich-quick schemes for the simple fact that a shortcut to wealth is much more appealing than the long game. In January 2009, just a month after Madoff's scandal was splashed across the headlines, a man named Nicolas Cosmo was charged by the CFTC for defrauding investors out of tens of millions of dollars. Cosmo promised his investors out-of-this-world returns of 50% per year. Much like Ponzi, Cosmo had previously been arrested for fraud but instead of going clean he opted to go for a bigger fraud the next time out.[14]

The reason Madoff's scam lasted so much longer than Ponzi's stamp fraud is that he wasn't promising to double people's money overnight. This was a more deliberate scam with the return numbers he falsified. Bernie Madoff preyed on people's fears and our inherent aversion to loss. Loss aversion is the idea that losses sting twice as bad as gains make us feel good. There's an entire literature of behavioral psychology research on the topic, but Andre Agassi explains this idea beautifully in his book, *Open: An Autobiography*, when discussing the difference between winning and losing on the biggest stage in professional tennis:

> But I don't feel that [winning] Wimbledon changed me. I feel, in fact, as if I've been let in on a dirty little secret: winning changes nothing. Now that I've won a slam, I know something that very few people on earth are permitted to know. A win doesn't feel as good as a loss feels bad, and the good feeling doesn't last as long as the bad. Not even close.[15]

Bernie's genius was promising returns of 10% to 12% year in and year out, something stock market investors would kill for. The made-up consistency of his investment returns even translated into his golf scores. Madoff always reported scores of between 80 and 89 for every round he played. Fraud was simply in this guy's DNA.[16] Reported numbers from one of the feeder funds that invested with Madoff shows just how unrealistic his reported performance numbers were. Over the course of 18 years, the fund earned nearly 11% per year, a decent return to be sure but not necessarily a grand slam. The eye-catching number is the reported volatility of this fund, which was just 2.5% with zero annual losses. To put this into context, the long-term volatility of the US stock market is roughly eight times higher than this. And not only were there no annual losses reported but nary a down quarter and just a few down months of performance.[17]

Madoff was promising all of the returns in the stock market with none of the risk. It's no wonder his investors never asked any questions. They assumed they'd hit the jackpot. So while his defrauded investors weren't greedy in the traditional sense, they were trying to skirt the sacred relationship that exists between risk and return by earning consistently high returns with very little volatility or loss. Bernie himself said, "Everyone was greedy. I just went along."[18]

Understanding the relationship between risk and return goes far beyond avoiding frauds and Ponzi schemes. Wall Street makes lots of money offering false promises that they can contain or completely eliminate risk from your portfolio. Risks can change shape but they never completely go away. If you wish to earn higher returns on your investments, occasionally you are going to have to suffer mind-numbing losses. If you wish to minimize mind-numbing losses on your investments, occasionally you are going to have to miss out on face-ripping gains. This is how risk and reward work. To those who think they have what it takes to break the bonds of this risk-reward relationship, to quote Jerry Seinfeld, "Good luck with all of that."

Notes

1. Bell A and Box D. Fraudster poses as Jason Statham to steal victim's money. BBC News [Internet]. 2019 Apr 29. Available from: https://www.bbc.com/news/uk-england-manchester-47969165
2. Bell C. 11 celebrities who got scammed by Bernie Madoff and lost millions. Bankrate [Internet]. 2017 May 17. Available from: https://www.bankrate.com/lifestyle/celebrity-money/11-celebrities-who-got-scammed-by-bernie-madoff-and-lost-millions/#slide=2
3. Greenspan S. *Annals of Gullibility: Why We Get Duped and How to Avoid It.* Westport, Connecticut: Praeger Publishers; 2009.
4. Greenspan S. Why we keep falling for financial scams. *The Wall Street Journal* [Internet]. 2009 Jan 3. Available from: https://www.wsj.com/articles/SB123093987596650197
5. Oakes K. The psychological trick explains how horoscopes can sound scarily accurate. *Science* [Internet]. 2018 Apr 26. Available from: https://inews.co.uk/news/science/barnum-effect-forer-horoscopes-accurate/
6. Train J. Famous financial fiascos. New York: Random House; 1984.
7. Darby M. In Ponzi we trust. Smithsonian.com [Internet] 1998 Dec. Available from: https://www.smithsonianmag.com/history/in-ponzi-we-trust-64016168/
8. Ibid.

9. Dunn D. Ponzi: *The Incredible True Story of the King of Financial Cons*. New York: Broadway Books; 2004.
10. Partnoy F. *The Match King: Ivar Kreuger, the Financial Genius Behind a Century of Wall Street Scandals*. New York: Public Affairs; 2009.
11. Train J. *Famous Financial Fiascos*. New York: Random House; 1984.
12. Dunn D. Ponzi: *The Incredible True Story of the King of Financial Cons*. New York: Broadway Books; 2004.
13. Greenspan S. Why we keep falling for financial scams. *The Wall Street Journal* [Internet]. 2009 Jan 3. Available from: https://www.wsj.com/articles/SB123093987596650197
14. U.S. Commodity Future Trading Commission. CFTC charges Nicholas Cosmo and Agape Companies with defrauding customers of tens of millions of dollars in commodity futures trading scheme. Release Number 56-6=09. 2009 Jan 27. Available from: https://www.cftc.gov/PressRoom/PressReleases/pr5606-09
15. Agassi A. *Open: An Autobiography*. New York: Vintage Books; 2010.
16. Seal M. Madoff's world. *Vanity Fair* [Internet]. 2009 Mar 4. Available from: https://www.vanityfair.com/news/2009/04/bernard-madoff-friends-family-profile
17. Portnoy B. *The Investor's Paradox: The Power of Simplicity in a World of Overwhelming Choice*. New York: Palgrave Macmillan; 2014.
18. Griffin T. A dozen things you can learn from the anti-models that are Bernard Madoff and his victims. 25iq [Internet]. 2016 Feb 13. Available from: https://25iq.com/2016/02/13/a-dozen-things-you-can-learn-from-the-anti-models-that-are-bernard-madoff-and-his-victims/

CHAPTER 14

The Easiest Person to Fool

All of humanity's problems stem from man's inability to sit quietly in a room alone.

—Blaise Pascal

When Cornelius Vanderbilt died in 1877 he was the richest person on the planet. Nicknamed "the Commodore" because of his vast shipping empire, Vanderbilt grew up poor and had little schooling but was a hard-nosed entrepreneur who built his fortune on the back of ownership and investments in waterway transport, railroads, and a host of other businesses. By the end of his life, the Commodore was worth more than $100 million, which would be the equivalent of an estimated $150 to $200 billion in today's dollars, making him one of the richest people to ever walk the earth. Unlike many from the Gilded Age following the industrial revolution, Vanderbilt was never interested in spending lavishly on himself, preferring instead to accumulate vast amounts of wealth. When he died he left his eldest son, William, the bulk of his estate.[1]

"Any fool can make a fortune," the Commodore advised William (whom he called Billy) before he died, but "it takes a man of brains to hold onto it after it is made." In the publishing business, this is what they call foreshadowing. Just six years after his father had passed away, Billy more than doubled his inheritance through some shrewd business deals and was now sitting on $194 million. Yet even after Billy doubled the family's money in short order, within 30 years of the death of his father, there wasn't a single heir or member of the Vanderbilt family who was among the richest people in America. Vanderbilt provided the initial gift to the university that bears his name in Nashville, TN. When 120 members of the family gathered at that university in 1973, not a single one of them was a millionaire.[2]

The Vanderbilts blew through their money the old-fashioned way – they spent it. Many people, myself included at one time, assume the Biltmore Estate in Asheville, NC was built as a shrine to the Commodore. Instead, it represents everything that went wrong with how the Vanderbilts managed to blow through their fortune. The mansion is the largest privately held home in the United States. Completed in 1895 for George Vanderbilt, one of Cornelius's many grandchildren and son to Billy, it took six years to build. The home measures nearly 180,000 square feet. Including the grounds, the estate sits on more than 8,000 acres of land. The house boasts over four acres of floor space with a total of 250 rooms, including 35 bedrooms, 45 bathrooms, and 65 fireplaces. There's a banquet hall with seven-story high ceilings, an indoor swimming pool that held 70,000 gallons of water, and a bowling alley.[3]

The land the home was built on was 146,000 acres or 228 square miles. It would take a person on horseback a week to make it around the entire border of the property line. Not only did the Biltmore cost an obscene amount of money to construct, but the upkeep and maintenance required began to bleed George dry just five years after it was finished. He died at age 52 with less than $1 million to his name after all his debts were settled.

After Billy died his $200 million fortune was divvied up among the family and summarily destroyed. The Biltmore was the most glaring show of opulence, but far from the only one. The family paid $3 million for a house built on Fifth Avenue in New York City. Parties thrown by millionaires at that house and around the city were otherworldly, costing upwards of $250,000 for a single shindig. And remember, this was the 1920s. That would be the equivalent of around $3 million today. For a party! At one party the hostess handed guests cigarettes rolled in $100 bills. People in the Gilded Age were literally lighting money on fire.

Willie Vanderbilt spent $500,000 on a yacht. The boat was so imposing that during an Atlantic Ocean voyage, a Turkish warship mistakenly fired shots across its bow. On a trip to Maine, Willie hit another boat because of a thick fog, sending his half a million dollar yacht to the bottom of the ocean. Instead of letting his wife know what had happened, his first message after the accident was to the shipyard to have them immediately begin construction on a new yacht, only this one was to be bigger, better, and more expensive.

Marble House is a gorgeous mansion the family built in Newport, Rhode Island, where anyone who was anyone with money summered at the time. It cost $2 million to build with an additional $9 million to decorate the interior. None of the children wanted the house because it was such a huge money suck, so it was sold at the depths of the Great Depression in 1932 for just $100,000. Another Vanderbilt grandchild built a summer home with his wife. It cost $7 million, plus millions more to furnish and decorate the interior. They would only spend one summer at the home. Of the dozens of luxurious mansions built by the Vanderbilt grandchildren, not a single one was used by the next generation.

The family had a fleet of Rolls Royces, many of which they never drove. By the 1940s, the house on Fifth Avenue, which cost $3 million to build, was assessed for just $175,000. Their collection of 183 paintings was purchased for more than $2 million. All 183 paintings, the "very best foreign paintings money could buy," garnered just over $323,000 when they were auctioned off in 1945. In trying to secure their place on the social hierarchy of the richest of the rich, the third generation of the Vanderbilts destroyed the world's largest fortune. No amount of money or material possessions could keep them happy.

After building on his father's fortune, Billy Vanderbilt admitted the following about a neighbor:

> He isn't worth a hundredth part as much as I am, but he has more of the real pleasures of life than I have. His house is as comfortable as mine, even if it didn't cost so much; his team is about as good as mine; his opera box is next to mine; his health is better than mine, and he will probably outlive me. And he can trust his friends.[4]

Being the richest person in the world brought more anxiety than happiness. To paraphrase his father, staying rich is often much harder than getting rich for people of means.

Getting Rich versus Staying Rich

The *Forbes* 400 list of the world's richest people seems to look fairly similar at the top every year. Buffett, Gates, Bezos, Bloomberg, and the Walton family have been at the top of the list in some order year after year for some time now (they've been joined by Mark Zuckerberg in recent years as well). But this list isn't as stable as it may appear. In the 33 *Forbes* 400 lists between 1982 and 2014, there were only 24 names that appeared on every single list. Just 34 names that were on the original 1982 list were still there by 2014. If we were to include families, 69 made it from the inaugural list until 2014, and those families made up almost 40% of the entire wealth of the 2014 list. Looking at this from another angle, that means the other 60% would be made up of newly created wealth over those three-plus decades. It's an impressive feat for those 69 families on the inaugural list to remain there for so long when so many others failed to keep up, but it's worth noting the annual wealth erosion from the original amount was in the order of 4% per year. If you take the data back even further we can see that the Vanderbilts' situation was the norm, not the outlier.

Half-life is a scientific measure that looks at the amount of time it takes for radioactive material to deteriorate to half of its original value. Wealth, it would seem, has a half-life of its own. The top 10 families by wealth in 1918, 1930, 1957, and 1968 saw their wealth cut in half in 13 years, 10 years, 13 years, and 8 years, respectively. There's an old saying that the first generation builds the wealth, the second generation maintains it, and the third generation spends it. Research shows this saying may be too lenient to the second generation. Grouping the top 30 members of the *Forbes* 400 list by generation, Arnott, Bernstein, and Wu found it was the first generation that maintained their wealth over their lifetimes, but the second generation saw a half-life of 24 years, while it took the grandkids just 11 years to cut their inheritance in half.[5]

High-income earners have a similarly difficult time staying at the top. Research shows over 50% of Americans will find themselves in the top 10% of earners for at least one year of their lives. More than 11% will find themselves in the top 1% of income-earners at some point. And close to 99% of those who make it into the top 1% of earners will find themselves on the outside looking in within a decade.[6]

Many people would give their pinky finger for a chance to have this kind of wealth or earn this type of money, even if it's only for a short period of time. And even losing half of your fortune when you're on the *Forbes* 400 list still leaves you in a better position than 99.9% of the world. No one should shed a tear when the wealthiest people in the world see their riches destroyed. Don't get me wrong, getting rich is no easy feat. In fact, it's estimated that just 5% of all Americans are millionaires.[7]

But you could make the claim that getting rich can be one of the worst things that could happen to you if your goal is preserving wealth. Success can beget more success but it can also sow the seeds of its own demise. Even Alanis Morrissette would find it ironic that getting rich is one of the biggest hurdles to staying rich because ego becomes your biggest enemy when you begin to outperform your past self in terms of money.

Shot out of a Cannon

Hunter S. Thompson burst onto the scene as a young journalist in the 1960s by getting "stomped" by the Hell's Angels. Thompson infiltrated the biker gang and spent time carousing with the group of outlaws for a year or so. His time with the bikers was cut short when he berated a member of the gang for beating his wife, which earned him a "stomping" from the group, thus ending his time researching the notorious biker gang. Thompson went on to write for *Rolling Stone* and a host of other publications, but he was best known for his 1971 book, *Fear and Loathing in Las Vegas*.[8]

Thompson died from a self-inflicted gunshot wound in 2005. Per his wishes, Thompson's ashes were blown into the sky by a 153-foot cannon as a crowd of mourners watched from below. The mourners included celebrities such as Bill Murray, Jack Nicholson, Benicio del Toro, John Cusack, Sean Penn, and Johnny Depp. When the movie version of *Fear and Loathing in Las Vegas* came out in 1998, Depp played the main character, Raoul Duke, who was based on Thompson's alter ego. Depp and Thompson became close friends to the point that the actor paid for many of the funeral arrangements on Thompson's behalf.[9]

When it was later reported Depp had spent $3 million on the cannon used to fire Thompson's ashes into the sky, the actor balked, telling *Rolling Stone* in an interview, "By the way, it was not $3 million to shoot Hunter into the f*cking sky. It was $5 million." Depp claims the cost of the cannon escalated because he wanted the arc of the ashes to be higher than the Statue of Liberty, which stands at 151 feet tall. In that same interview, Depp set the record straight on other financial matters, as well. There was another story that reported Depp was spending upwards of $30,000 a month on wine. Depp would not let this injustice stand either. His retort was, "It's insulting to say that I spent $30,000 on wine because it was far more."[10]

These are absurd financial matters to get worked up about, and you would assume one would want to shy away from bragging about wasting so much money. But when you're a world-famous actor who earned nearly two-thirds of $1 billion in your career on such hits as the *Pirates of the Caribbean* franchise and *Alice in Wonderland*, surely this type of spending shouldn't make a difference, right? That's pocket change. Well, that pocket change can add up even when we're talking about a fabulously wealthy actor. A few million for a chateau in France here, a few million for a chain of four islands in the Bahamas there – sprinkle in 40 full-time employees ($300,000/month), 24-hour security for his entire family ($150,000/month), and a luxurious yacht with a crew and maintenance ($300,000–$400,000/month) and, eventually, we're talking about real money, even with someone who has career earnings approaching $700 million.

The details of Depp's profligate spending habits came to light in part because he sued The Management Group (TMG), who was responsible for overseeing the movie star's business affairs. Depp sought $25 million for negligence, fraud, unjust enrichment, and breach of fiduciary duty. The actor alleged the company mismanaged his money for almost two decades, didn't keep proper financial records, and failed to pay his taxes on time. TMG countersued, claiming the actor lived a "selfish, reckless, and irresponsible lifestyle." TMG said Depp, "Caused his own financial waste."[11]

The suit was quickly settled out of court, and no details were released on the amount of the settlement or who was to blame.

The Biggest Fraud of All

You'll notice the stories in this chapter aren't like the other financial frauds described elsewhere in this book. It's possible TMG committed some sort of fraud or negligence when dealing with Depp's finances but even if his managers did defraud the actor in some way, the biggest financial scam here was the one Depp committed against his own self-interests. Richard Feynman once said, "The first principle is that you must not fool yourself and you are the easiest person to fool." The biggest financial fraud of all is often the financial pain we inflict on ourselves through poor decisions, bad habits, and self-delusion. Sometimes the biggest charlatan is the person looking back at us in the mirror.

The mistakes made by the Vanderbilt family and Johnny Depp are nothing new. The details may change but the story of someone making a boatload of dough only to see their lifestyle outstrip their riches is as old as time. Nor are these actions exclusive of the ultra-wealthy class. There is a huge difference between making lots of money and being rich. Income is not the same thing as wealth. Those who earn a high income give themselves a better chance of becoming rich, but there is far more temptation to inject extreme lifestyle inflation into the mix when you earn a bigger paycheck. Emails that came to light through the lawsuit showed the actor, who was paid upwards of $20 million a picture, was basically living paycheck to paycheck. Depp said, "I'm not a lawyer. I'm not an accountant. I'm not qualified to help my 15-year-old son with his math homework…I've always trusted the people around me."[12]

Depp also said, "Wine is not an investment if you drink it as soon as you buy it." This is a good way to think about income as well. If you spend it all as soon as you earn it, you'll never get ahead financially. Your net worth is the difference between what you own and what you owe. You can think of spending less than you make as what you own and spending more than you make as what you owe. The difference between how much you make and how much you spend is often a tug of war between ego and humility. Unfortunately, for many people ego wins out when it comes to spending money.

Anyone can act rich. Acting rich isn't that hard. You know what's hard? Acting like you're not rich even when you make a decent chunk of change. After the initial rush from new circumstances, such as making more money, people become accustomed to their new situation. A good way to give yourself a margin of safety is to assume your current financial situation won't last forever. There are plenty of ways to get rich – start a business, save and invest wisely, inherit money, get lucky, etc. But staying rich involves just a few simple variables – self-awareness, modesty, and the ability to delay gratification with a portion of your capital. Money can corrupt even the best of intentions. No matter how much you make, you still must save and live below your means to build sustainable wealth.

All that stuff Depp bought with his money sounds great. Who wouldn't like to own a chateau or their own island or a fully-staffed yacht or, heck, even a $5 million cannon they can use to shoot their friends' remains into the ether? But true wealth is the absence of stuff. Saving is the spending that never occurred because you decided to delay gratification to spend it later. There's nothing wrong with spending money on the things that are important in your life, but to truly build wealth you must be willing to forego some things that aren't as important.

If you can't prioritize your spending habits, you'll never be able to save enough to get ahead, no matter how much money you earn.

Notes

1. The 20 richest people of all time. Lovemoney.com [Internet]. 2017 Apr 25. Available from: https://www.msn.com/en-in/money/photos/the-20-richest-people-of-all-time/ss-BBsg8nX#image=8
2. Vanderbilt II AT. *Fortune's Children: The Fall of the House of Vanderbilt.* New York: William Morrow; 2013.
3. The Biltmore. Available from: https://www.biltmore.com/
4. Vanderbilt II AT. *Fortune's Children: The Fall of the House of Vanderbilt.* New York: William Morrow; 2013.
5. Arnott R, Wu L, and Bernstein WJ. The myth of dynastic wealth: the rich get poorer. Cato Journal. 2015 Fall;35(3):447–45. Available from: https://www.researchaffiliates.com/en_us/publications/journal-papers/359_the_myth_of_dynastic_wealth_the_rich_get_poorer.html
6. Follet C. High turnover among America's rich. Cato Institute [Internet] 2016 Jan 8. Available from: https://www.cato.org/blog/high-turn-over-among-americas-rich
7. Wile R. 1 out of every 20 Americans is now a millionaire: report. *Money* [Internet]. 2017 Nov 14. Available from: http://money.com/money/5023038/millionaire-population-united-states-world
8. Barnett D. Hunter S Thompson: how we need the godfather of gonzo today, served up with his side order of guns, booze and drugs. Independent [Internet]. 2018 Jan 20. Available from: https://www.independent.co.uk/news/long_reads/hunter-s-thompson-death-suicide-kill-himself-how-die-gonzo-journalism-warren-hinckle-a8161841.html
9. Ashes of Hunter S. Thompson blown into sky. *The New York Times* [Internet]. 2005 Aug 21. Available from: https://www.nytimes.com/2005/08/21/world/americas/ashes-of-hunter-s-thompson-blown-into-sky.html

10. Rodrick S. The trouble with Johnny Depp. *Rolling Stone* [Internet]. 2018 Jun 21. Available from: https://www.rollingstone.com/movies/movie-features/the-trouble-with-johnny-depp-666010/

11. Ibid.

12. Bryant K. Johnny Depp lived from giant paycheck to giant paycheck, apparently. *Vanity Fair* [Internet]. 2017 Jun 20. Available from: https://www.vanityfair.com/style/2017/06/johnny-depp-lawsuit-emails-pay-check-to-paycheck

Conclusion:

Six Signs of Financial Fraud

There is no real substitute for common sense – except for good luck, which is a substitute for everything.

—Jim Simons

Fraud can happen anywhere at any time because no matter the state of the world, there will always be con artists, hucksters, and charlatans who know how to sell the path to easy riches. And, unfortunately, there will always be people willing to take the other side of that trade. I came across a number of data sources that estimated the amount of money lost to financial fraud each year and the number of people who get scammed out of their money. But the truth is those numbers are always on the low side because there are so many people who get taken advantage of who never report what happened to them because they're embarrassed. They're embarrassed because they believed in someone or something that was obviously a scam with the benefit of hindsight, but that they glossed over in the moment.

Because financial fraud is never going away, you must prepare yourself to detect red flags that may arise when listening to an investment pitch. Many warning signs appear clear as day only in hindsight because money often blinds us in the moment from tapping into our common sense. Here are six signs of financial fraud:

1. The Money Manager Has Custody of Your Assets

If you wanted to find a single reason for how Bernie Madoff was able to fool so many people en route to a $65 billion Ponzi scheme, look

163

no further than the fact that he had custody of client assets. This means Madoff's firm personally held his client's money, a big no-no. You always want to separate the decision-maker of the investments and the custody of assets. Any reputable money manager or financial advisor should hold the assets of their clients at a third-party bank or outside financial institution. This drastically reduces the risk that a client's money will get stolen or used as a personal piggy bank of the investment manager.

A multibillion-dollar fund would typically work with a number of financial intermediaries to execute the strategy from an operational perspective. This would include several brokers to execute trades and ensure trading costs were competitive, a fund administrator to calculate and report on the market value of the portfolio, and a bank custodian to actually hold the assets on behalf of the investors. Madoff's operation performed all of these tasks in house with zero oversight from a third party. They didn't use an independent custodian which basically gave him free rein to alter client statements, manipulate returns, send out false reports, defy auditors, and do what he pleased with client funds. The reason Bernie is in custody (behind bars) is because he had custody (of assets). And I'll show myself out.

To do list: Ask your financial advisor or investment manager who has custody of your assets. Make sure it's an independent third party who allows your investment advisor to trade on your behalf but not transfer funds into and out of your account without your prior authorization.

2. There Is an Aura of Exclusivity in the Pitch

The rich and powerful are different than most people when it comes to managing money because, well, they have more of it. One of the best sales pitches to the wealthy class is making it sound like an exclusive deal because many rich people like to believe they're special. There are no shortcuts when it comes to investing your money. Good investing is typically boring. But if you're able to promote exclusivity, that tends to perk people's ears up a little.

Professional investors like to tout their "proprietary methodology" or "the select group of investors chosen for an exclusive deal" or the "secret wealth-building strategy no one else knows about" or "getting you in on the ground floor." These types of sales pitches make us feel good because we all want to believe we're a special snowflake when it comes to managing our life savings. We deserve the secret sauce, right?

Lloyd's of London is an insurance company in Great Britain that was founded in 1686. The firm has an aura prestige from their long history of working with British aristocrats. In the 1990s, the company touted their reputation as a sound, blue-chip institution to new investors in the United States who were looking for stable returns, and the ability to invest with an exclusive brand. The problem is these new investors were often attracted to the riskiest of insurance products, exposing them to enormous liabilities they couldn't possibly understand, which meant huge losses for many involved and a lawsuit for Lloyd's.[1]

To do list: Ask yourself why the person or firm is sharing an exclusive deal or investment or strategy with you. If it's so important to keep things a secret, why would they share it with you in the first place? Exclusivity may make a financial scheme *feel* more important and appealing, but the reality is 99.9% of the time it's just a sales pitch to get you to hand over your money quicker. Once-in-a-lifetime investment sales pitches tend to come along far more often than once-in-a-lifetime investment strategies that actually work as intended.

3. When the Strategy Is too Complicated to Understand

Will Rogers once said, "I would rather be the man who bought the Brooklyn Bridge than the man who sold it." Rogers was talking about George C. Parker, the con artist who somehow successfully "sold" the Brooklyn Bridge, along with a few other pieces of property he didn't own, to unsuspecting buyers. Unfortunately, when it comes to financial fraud, the number of people who are looking to buy the Brooklyn Bridge will always outnumber those looking to sell the Brooklyn Bridge. There will always be a market for these schemes because people are always in search of a shortcut for getting rich.

Making a fraud too complex to understand is one way to get people on board because (a) we all like to believe we're smart and don't want to look stupid by admitting we don't understand something and (b) it's much easier to be fooled by randomness when something is complicated or hard to understand.

A team of psychology researchers discovered most people who go to see a magician never want to find out how they pull off their magic tricks. Participants in one study were shown a host of magic tricks, including one where the magician made a helicopter disappear. Subjects were then given the opportunity to either get the full explanation about how they pulled it off or watch another magic trick. Surprisingly, 60% of people chose to watch another trick while just 40% asked to see how the illusion was performed.[2] It's almost as if people are drawn to mystery. We want to be fooled and there are plenty of people who are more than willing to oblige.

"Trust us, we got this" is the financial pitch of yesteryear, before people had the ability to actually look stuff up on the Internet. This premise rested on the idea that financial professionals know more than you, so just leave them be and let them do what they want with your money. The black box shouldn't fly anymore in the era of transparency. Professional money managers should be more informed than their clients when it comes to managing wealth, but they should also be able to explain their strategy or philosophy well enough that a 6-year-old could understand it. No legitimate investment strategy should be too murky, flashy, or complicated for clients to understand. The rich and powerful generally avoid the appearance of not understanding something because it makes them look weak. Don't let your ego get in the way of your financial health.

To do list: If someone either can't or won't divulge how they're managing your money that's a huge red flag. You can outsource your investments but never outsource your understanding of what's going on with your money. If it's too complicated to understand, don't invest in it.

4. When the Story Is too Good to Be True

General Gregor MacGregor was a Scottish war veteran in South America who pulled off one of the biggest, most diabolical cons of the nineteenth century. Well known for his promotional abilities, MacGregor convinced a large number of his fellow Scots he was the prince of Poyais, a country in Central American. MacGregor described a place with boundless opportunities to plant vegetables, where fruit grew as far as the eye could see, wild game was plentiful for hunting, and rivers were overflowing with gold.

Investors quickly handed over £200,000 in bonds to develop Poyais based on MacGregor's sales ability alone. Seven shiploads of people boarded boats to sail to a country that was a figment of a con man's imagination. The boats landed in Honduras, expecting to see a flourishing town, but instead found an uninhabitable landscape. Many of those people became sick or died from the poor living conditions.[3]

MacGregor used a combination of celebrity from his war exploits and the promise of riches during a time when a decent return on investment was difficult to come by. Somehow he was able to convince thousands of people of the existence of a fictional country thousands of miles away.

In 1908 a scammer posted the following ad in a handful of newspapers:

> This is not fake – it does not ask you to speculate, to gamble, nor to canvass. You can do it at home. Five dollars becomes ten – ten dollars becomes twenty dollars. It is absolutely sure, and if you do not prove it true to yourself within a week after we send you our secret we will return your money. The wealthiest men of the country have tried it and succeeded. For two dollars ($2) we will send your secret. Remember, if you find it fails within a week you can have your two dollars back.

Thousands of people sent in their $2 with the hopes of learning how to double their money through this secret. They were sent a reply reading: "Convert your money into bills, and fold them."[4] If it sounds too good to be true…you know the rest.

To do list: Stress-test every financial idea or strategy that comes your way by formulating arguments against the idea. Perform a pre-mortem to figure out what could potentially go wrong in advance to help yourself see what you could be missing in the moment. If the returns sound too good to be true, they probably are. If the investment pitch is too good to be true, it probably is. If the promises of riches sound too good to be true, they probably are.

5. When the Returns Are Ridiculously Good

William Franklin Miller worked in a brokerage house in the late 1800s, gaining clients by telling them he had "insider tips." Through these tips, he marketed an astounding 10% return. But these returns weren't promised over the course of a year, they were promised over the course of a week. That's a cool 520% per year! As is often the case with such lofty promises, Miller never actually did anything with the money.

Instead, his main job was spreading the word about his fraudulent investment scheme. He even printed newsletters that read "My ambition is to make the Franklin Syndicate one of the largest and strongest syndicates operating in Wall Street, which will enable us to manipulate stocks, putting them up or down as we desire, and which will make our profits five times more than they are now." Securities laws were pretty lax back then, but it takes a lot of nerve to blatantly advertise the fact that you're going to try to manipulate the market. And the worst part is he was never even trying to actually manipulate the market! It was a Ponzi scheme, pure and simple. This scheme began bringing in something like $80,000 a day. Because he was advertising market manipulation right in his marketing materials, it didn't take long for the authorities to start looking into his scheme. Miller fled to Canada when the scheme was discovered by the authorities and his "investors" were left holding the bag (which was of course empty).[5]

High promised returns will always suck people in because everyone wants to believe unicorns exist in the financial world. Always remind yourself of the following – if someone could honestly produce consistently enormous returns every week, month, or year, why would they offer you the opportunity to profit with them in the first place? If they truly could earn such fantastic returns, they wouldn't need to or want to tell anyone else about the secret sauce.

To do list: Be realistic about the level of returns you can earn on any investment you may be pursuing. Do some research to figure out what a reasonable rate of return is and look beyond a sales pitch anytime someone promises you certain return numbers. Anything that's too high or too consistent is a red flag. Proceed with caution anytime someone makes promises about the future in terms of what your returns will be, especially if they sound too good to be true.

6. When They Tell You Exactly What You Want to Hear

While working hard to discredit medical quack John Brinkley (see Chapter 1), Morris Fishbein of the American Medical Association described three qualities of a charlatan to help others understand how they operate:

1. **They wrap themselves inside legends, half-truths, and a grand lie.** For Brinkley this meant positioning himself against the

medical establishment, selling miracle cures and an alternative to true science.

2. **They are extremely selfish.** Brinkley never shared his secret medical miracles with any other health professionals, which was a huge red flag because a true doctor would share their results for peer review.

3. **They are master manipulators.** Charlatans tell people exactly what they want to hear and sell hope to prey on people's emotions.[6]

The easiest way to manipulate others is through storytelling ability. The acclaimed book *Sapiens: A Brief History of Human Kind* by Yuval Harari describes how humans made the leap from relatively tiny groups of simple hunter-gatherers to the more complex modern world full of enormous cities, cultures, groups, and organizations. It wasn't necessarily a technological breakthrough that did the trick but our ability to tell stories:

> How did Homo sapiens manage to cross this critical threshold, eventually founding cities comprising tens of thousands of inhabitants and empires ruling hundreds of millions? The secret was probably the appearance of fiction. Large numbers of strangers can cooperate successfully by believing in common myths.

Telling effective stories is not easy, which is why it's so difficult for many to spot a fraud even when it's staring them in the face. These people are wonderful at selling themselves through the power of story. In her book *The Confidence Game,* Maria Konnikova shares why we so easily ignore facts but take a story at face value, "When a fact is plausible, we still need to test it. When a story is plausible, we often assume it's true." She argues that when we hear a good story we almost immediately let our guard down. How else could you explain something like the Nigerian Prince scam? Or the airplane game? Or a doctor that claimed to cure men's virility by surgically implanting goat testicles into their scrotums? Or a multibillion-dollar Ponzi scheme where no one ever loses money? Stories stick with us while facts and figures do not.

To do list: Every fraud in history has had a wonderful story attached to it. The people hurt by those frauds never bothered to check the legitimacy of those stories. Do your own homework and don't take anyone's story at face value simply because you want to believe it. Stories are nice, but verifying the evidence behind any story where money is involved can help save you from yourself.

Notes

1. Griffin R and Inman P. How the Names lost their shirts: the background Lloyd's in court. *The Guardian* [Internet]. 2000 Nov 3. Available from: https://www.theguardian.com/money/2000/nov/04/business.personalfinancenews1

2. Kuhn, G. *Experiencing the Impossible: The Science of Magic.* Cambridge, MA: MIT Press; 2019.

3. Tattersall I and Névraumont P. *Hoax: A History of Deception: 5,000 years of Fakes, Forgeries, and Fallacies.* New York: Running Press; 2018.

4. Nash JR. *Hustlers and Con Men: An Anecdotal History of the Confidence Man and His Games.* New York: M. Evans & Company; 1976.

5. Ibid.

6. Dunphy S. 'Every man his own doctor': probing public health and medical quackery in U.S. historical newspapers and government publications. The Readex Blog [Internet]. 2017 Apr 12. Available from: https://www.readex.com/blog/%E2%80%98every-man-his-own-doctor%E2%80%99-probing-public-health-and-medical-quackery-us-historical-newspapers

Index